THE
DISSERTATION COOKBOOK

FROM SOUP TO NUTS

A PRACTICAL GUIDE TO
HELP YOU START AND COMPLETE
YOUR DISSERTATION OR RESEARCH PROJECT

Marilyn K. Simon, Ph.D. and J. Bruce Francis, Ph.D.

KENDALL/HUNT PUBLISHING COMPANY
4050 Westmark Drive   Dubuque, Iowa 52002

Changes in the Second Edition

The Second Edition of the Dissertation Cookbook includes many familiar and new features intended to guide you through the research process in a positive and supportive way, and to assuage any concerns you might have about any aspect of doing quality contributory research.

In response to extensive surveys, focus groups, and in-depth reviewer feedback, every phase of the Dissertation Cookbook has been carefully revised and fully edited to ensure appropriate content coverage and the highest degree of accuracy.

Highlights of Content Changes

* More attention has been given to developing the research proposal and the problem statement.
* More information regarding both quantitative and qualitative analyses.
* More information regarding research methodologies.
* Expanded glossaries of important terms has been included.
* Expanded bibliography of recommended and referenced books has been included.
* More information on technology integration.

Research is a systematic, structured, purposeful, and disciplined process of discovery. Since each type of knowledge is unique, the Dissertation Cookbook presents a variety of systematic methods to access different types of knowledge. If your research is carefully planned and conducted, and contains the appropriate ingredients, an analysis of data will produce valuable descriptions and inferences about the phenomenon you are investigating. Following the recommended "recipe" will enable you to "relish" in the entire procedure.

The Dissertation Cookbook will guide you through the preliminary preparation of your research, the research process itself, and assist you in reporting your findings so that others can benefit from the "fruits" of your labor. In this way you will be able to make valuable contributions to the knowledge base of your field of study.

TABLE OF CONTENTS

PHASE 1—PLANNING YOUR FEAST: GETTING STARTED

PROCEED [7 Easy Steps to a Great Start] 2
  Possess a Positive Attitude 3
  Read Efficiently 6
  Organize Your Time 9
  Creating a Working Environment 12
  Extend Your Note-taking and Writing Skills 12
    Record Keeping 12
    Mind Mapping 14
    PIE Writing 15
  Enter Information Into a Computer, Journal or Tape Deck 16
  Design a Survival Kit 18
PICK YOUR REPAST [Choose Your Topic] 19
  Possess Knowledge of What a Dissertation Is and Is Not 19
  Identifying Your Style 20
  Classify Yourself Professionally 24
  K (C)onduct the ROC Bottom Test 26
CLASSIFY YOUR REPAST—What's Cooking? [Identify Your Study] 32
  Past Perspective 33
    Historical Research 33
    Causal-Comparative Research 34
    Content Analysis 34
  Present Perspective 35
    Developmental Research 35
    Descriptive Research 36
    Correlational 36
    Pure/Basic/Experimental Research 37
    Case Study 38
    Phenomenology 38
  Future Perspective 39
    Applied or Evaluative Research 39
    Action Research 40
  "Nouveau Cuisine" 41
    Heuristic Research 41
    Holistic Research 42
    Grounded Theory 43
    Ethnographic 44
    Delphi Research Technique 45
  Qualitative/Quantitative 46
    A Test of Your Research Acumen 47

BE AWARE OF HEALTH HAZARDS [Ethics of Research]   48
    Responsibility   49
    Competence   53
    Moral and Legal Issues   53
    Proper Representation   54
    What Can Be Done?   55
CHOOSE YOUR ATTIRE [Form and Style]   56

PHASE 2—ACCOUTREMENTS

UTENSILS [Choosing Your Instruments]   59
    Pre-Packaged Tests and Inventories   59
    Questionnaires   62
    Adjuncts to Questionnaires   71
        Pilot Study   71
        Cover Letter   71
        Going the Extra Mile   74
    The Personal Interview   75
    Observation   77
SERVING PLATTERS/SPICES [Statistics]   79
    What's Stat ? (you say?)   79
    The Role of Statistics   80
    Frequently Asked Questions About Statistics   81
    How to Exhibit Your Date (a)   85
ASSISTANT CHEFS   88
    Choosing Your Sample   88
    Sampling Error   92
    Confidence Levels   92
HOW TO (AP)PRAISE YOUR DATE (A)   93
    Statistical Hypothesis Testing   94
    Testing a Claim About a Mean   95
    Testing Claims About 2 Means   108
    Testing Claims About 3 or More Means (ANOVA)   110
    Testing a Claim About Proportions/Percentages   115
    Testing Claims About Standard Deviations and Variability   117
    Testing a Claim About the Relation Between Two Variables   119
    Multivariate Correlation Statistics   127
    Analysis of Covariance (ANCOVA)   130
    Contingency Tables   131
    Statistical Terms   133
    Test Your Research Acumen   138
    The 4 P's (Preliminary Preparation: Proposal Planning)   139

PHASE 3—THE FEAST

CHAPTER 1—APPETIZER   141
    Introduction   141
    The Problem Statement   143
    Background   146
    Purpose   148
    Significance   149
    Nature of the Study   151
    Hypotheses/Research Questions   153
    Scope and Limitations   155
    Definitions   155
CHAPTER 2—SOUP/SALAD   157
    Research/Literature Review (LEADS)   157
CHAPTER 3/CHAPTER 4—MAIN COURSE   163
    Methodology—What Did You Do?   163
    Presentation and Analysis of Data   165
CHAPTER 5—DESSERT   170
    Conclusions, Implications, and Recommendations   170
ABSTRACT   171
SUGGESTED READINGS   173
INDEX   178

To the Turners
whose vision of Walden University enables
students and staff to adhere to Thoreau's advice and:
*"Direct our eyes inward for there we find a thousand
regions of our mind yet undiscovered."*

```
┌─────────────────────────────────────────────────────────┐
│                      PHASE 1                             │
│                                                          │
│         Planning Your Feast--Getting Started             │
│                                                          │
│         PROCEED [7 Easy Steps to a Great Start]          │
│                                                          │
│         PICK YOUR REPAST [Choose Your Topic]             │
│                                                          │
│      CLASSIFY YOUR REPAST--"WHAT'S COOKING?"             │
│                                                          │
│              [Identify Your Study]                       │
│                                                          │
│   BE AWARE OF HEALTH HAZARDS [Ethics of Research]        │
│                                                          │
│         CHOOSE YOUR ATTIRE [Form and Style]              │
│                                                          │
└─────────────────────────────────────────────────────────┘
```

Putting together an excellent dissertation is like planning and preparing a gourmet feast for a gathering of distinguished guests. The student-researcher could think of him/her self as the chef and chief meal engineer for this elegant repast.

Congratulations! By securing your copy of the Dissertation Cookbook and reading this information, you have taken an important first step to secure the successful realization of your goal--you have shown an interest. Your next step is to turn your interest into result-getting actions.

The following ingredients are part of your Dissertation Cookbook's recipe for an excellent beginning to an excellent "feast" (dissertation/research paper). An acronym, decree, and seven step recipe that will insure your initial and ultimate success is:

PROCEED!

1 cup	**P** ossess a Positive Attitude
1 cup	**R** ead Efficiently
1 cup	**O** rganize Your Time
1 cup	**C** reate a Space to Work
1 cup	**E** xtend Your Note taking and Writing Skills
1 cup	**E** nter Information onto a Computer, Tape Deck or Journal
1 cup	**D** esign a Survival Kit

1cup(c) "P"ossess a Positive Attitude

mix with a dash of each: visualization, exercise, determination, and sound nutrition. Remember: Your *attitudes shape your future!*

It is important that you are obtaining your degree for **you,** and that you work on a research project that **you,** as well as your advisors and mentors, are enthusiastic about.

Arnold Schwarzenegger, five-time Mr. Universe and four-time Mr. Olympic, told reporters, "*As long as your mind can envision that you can do something; then you can do it.*"

The following activities will enable you to use **visualization** techniques to assist you in creating and maintaining a positive attitude through the successful completion of your dissertation or research project.

1. Visualize yourself successfully producing an excellent dissertation.

2. Imagine enjoying each aspect of creating your dissertation or research project.

3. Conjure up an image of yourself working in a pleasant environment, accomplishing goals that you will see your project to fruition.

4. Picture yourself obtaining the degree and recognition you are seeking.

5. Repeat these steps each time you begin work on your dissertation/research project.

Fill out the information on the cutting board to further assist you in visualizing your preparation of an outstanding "feast."

cutting board:

1.   Take a few minutes to reflect upon the benefits you will receive upon the successful completion of your goal.

What are some of those benefits? _____
_____

2.   Take a look at the table of contents (iii),PHASE 3-THE FEAST [Your Dissertation]. These are the ingredients (Chapters) that constitute most dissertations. Take a moment to digest this information.
Imagine what **your** dissertation will look like. Can you see it bound with your name and degree on the cover? ___ Will you have it hard bound or soft bound or both? _____ How many copies do you think you will make of your final dissertation text? _____

3.   Most dissertations are between 100 and 200 pages while research papers can be significantly less. Approximately how many pages do you envision your dissertation or research paper to be? _____

4.   Do you envision having graphs and charts? __ How many references do you think you will consult? _____

5.   What will change once you get your degree or finish your research?
_____

6.   Who will you tell about your successes?
_____

7.   What do you see as their reaction?
_____

8. If you are hoping to obtain a Ph.D., then the next time you call directory assistance introduce yourself as Dr. _____(surname) and see how that title feels to you.

Your body and mind are closely related. Your mental efficiency is affected by the state of your body. Check to see that your diet is healthful. Many studies suggest that protein helps keep the brain alert and that the brain's performance is also affected by choline (a B-complex vitamin that is found in egg yolks, beef liver, fish, raisins, and legumes). Other B vitamins as well as Vitamin C and iron are also essential in maintaining a healthy brain.

Stay away from alcohol during your dissertation working days. See to it that your exercise is efficient and enjoyable. The mental effects of regular exercise are profound and extensive, touching your intellect, memory, and emotions.

cutting board:

1. What in your diet needs to be improved to see that you have the best possible nutrition?

_____

_____

2. What type of exercise do you enjoy doing that could help you become more fit?

_____

3. What other measures can you take to support yourself in the successful obtainment of your goal?

_____

_____

4. Sleep is important for the renewed health of the brain. When you drift off into unconsciousness -- a procedure that happens in stages -- your brain goes through a series of psychological processes that restores both mind and body. At certain stages memories are consolidated and at other stages your brain is working out resolutions to unconscious conflicts. Certain factors such as the use of alcohol or drugs, a noisy bedroom, an uncomfortable bed, stress carried over from the day, or other disruptions, may upset this pattern.
Too much sleep can be as detrimental as too little sleep. Most adults do very well with 6-8 hours of sleep. How much sleep do you **really** need to feel great? ___ See that you get that amount during your research working days and try to eliminate any conditions that disrupt your sleep.

1c   "R"ead Efficiently
Understand Scholarly Language
The book exists for us perchance which will explain our miracles and reveal
new ones
Walden...Henry David Thoreau

Practically all research projects, and thus
dissertations, require a voluminous amount of reading from
texts, journals, periodicals, newspapers, web pages, etc. The
following tasks have been employed by successful
researchers to help make their reading   more productive.
Put an asterisk (*) next to the activities that you already
cultivate, and an exclamation mark (!) next to the ones that
you could employ to make *your* reading more constructive.
You will find more "helpful hints" in the Literature Review
Section of Phase 3. If you have already mastered the
information below, perhaps you should check out that
section now.

___1. Take time to reflect on what it is you are hoping
to find before you begin to read.

___2. Survey the table of contents and note major
headings.

___3. If there are chapter summaries in a text, or an
abstract for a paper, read them before exploring the
chapter or paper.

___4. As you read, try to relate the information to
something you are already familiar with.

___5. Take notes or highlight important ideas. If you
can do this at the keyboard you can save yourself
quite a bit of time.

___6. Check for patterns that the author might be
applying such as:

Cause and effect -- the author explains a situation or theory and then delves into the consequences of its application.

Compare/Contrast -- the author examines two or more different theories or situations and their relationship to each other.

Process-description -- a concept, program, or project is delineated and then examples are provided.

Sequential -- a case is built in a linear or historical manner.

__7. Be an active reader: always ask yourself questions about what you are reading such as: What is the author's purpose? Why am I reading this? What conclusions does the author come to? Is this reasonable? Who else supports this view?

__8. Imagine that the author is personally speaking with you (just like **your** Dissertation Cookbook does).

In order to cope with the demands of a discipline, one must be able to grasp the implications of important concepts that permeate the literature. For example, in reading scholarly works one frequently comes across terms such as *paradigm, theory, validity, bias,* etc. It is important to understand the meaning of these terms in the context in which they are found. Many of these important terms can be found in various sections of your Dissertation Cookbook.

Scholarly language is a specialized form of discourse which helps frame what is considered to be the limits of acceptable scholarly practices, philosophies, and purposes. It is governed by logic at the most abstract level of critical analysis. When you write in an academic manner, you are identified as a "member of the community of scholars." What you write can be substantiated by those who "consume" what you write. Scholarly literacy is a moving target, and it is thus crucial that you keep up with the professional literature *after* you have obtained your degree.

The rationale for using this rarefied language is that it can capture complexity and distinctiveness of processes that cannot easily be described in colloquial terms. It also enables academicians to express ideas more forcefully and intelligently, and helps eliminate ambiguity. A negative effect is that it can also be used (intentionally or unintentionally) to intimidate those "not in the club."

The following adages illustrate both the beauty and the bafflement one encounters in scholarly discourse. These two "simple statements" epitomize how brevity can belie the complexity inherent in the language of the scholar. Determine which "camp" you are in, or under which conditions you favor one philosophy over the other. Practice saying these expressions and sharing them with a friend. This will make you sound like a true scholar.

Camp 1: *Epistemology presupposes ontology*

This is the realist view which contends that in order to know (episteme) there must be something real (ontos) to know. It is a belief favored by those who employ quantitative methodologies. Members of this *camp* contend there is a "solution" to a problem that can be found using the scientific method of deduction.

Camp 2: *Ontology presupposes epistemology*

This is the constructivist view which contends that our knowing (episteme) gives reality its realness (ontos). It is a belief held by postmodernists and constructivists who purport that there is no *one* reality and that context is everything. Qualitative methodologists support this notion and believe that reality is socially constructed through individual or collective definitions of the situation. This philosophy is more concerned with understanding and consistency than in trying to explain a phenomenon. Members of this *camp* contend that conclusions are based on induction and context sensitivity, and that universal, context-free generalizations are non-existent.

cutting board:

     1. Which of the active reading strategies above do you already employ? ___
     2. Which of these suggestions do you need to practice? ___
     3. Which of the two "camps" are you a member of? _____
Why? _____

1c "O" rganize your time

By planning your future, you can live in the present...Time is one of your most valuable resources, and it is important that you spend it wisely.
Lee Berglund...founder of Personal Resource Systems

An excellent first step in effective time and activity management is to write down your goals. On the cutting board below write down the day that you plan to complete your dissertation (or research project); "DCD" or "RCD." (You might want to do this after you have completed PHASE1 of your Dissertation Cookbook).

cutting board:

     My D(R)CD will be _____ (date). At that time I will have successfully completed the written part of my dissertation/research project and sent it to the proper authorities.

     Next, it is important that you recognize other things that you *have* to do and *want* to do between now and "D(R)CD."

On the cutting board below write down the things in your life that you **have to do** and then the things that are not on the list that you **want to do** between now and "D(R)CD."

cutting board:

1. I have to do the following activities between now and D(R)CD:

_____
_____

2. In addition I want to do the following activities:

_____
_____

Good Job! Now let us break this down into smaller chunks and make a plan for next week. First, fill in the following calendar with all the time that you will be attending to your "have to's." Next, fill in quality time that you can dedicate to your research. Choose something that you want to do that is not on the schedule, and plan for that as well.

MON	TUES	WED	THURS	FRI	SAT	SUN

cutting board:

1. Make an affirmation for the next seven days.

* By _____I will have achieved the following goals in my research:

_____

_____
_____

2. Make an affirmation for the next month.

By _____I will have achieved the following
goals in my research: _____
_____
_____

* Begin each new week with a similar affirmation until "DCD."

There are many activities that you can do to support yourself in the preparation and serving of your feast. You may want to learn how to use the computer in a university library, learn how to do on-line searches on the internet, or purchase a new or used computer. You may need to learn a new program, obtain supplies, research a variety of preliminary topics, take a refresher course in statistics at a local college, consult with advisors in your field or in other fields, relieve yourself from a prior responsibility, etc.

On the cutting board below, make a list of five things that will support you in completing your research by D(R)CD, and times that you will be able to attend to these things.

cutting board:

By _____(date) I will : _____
By _____(date) I will : _____
By _____(date) I will : _____
By _____(date) I will : _____
By _____(date) I will : _____

1 c "C"reating a Working Environment

Your own space-- a little time with your own thoughts in (your) own space...where there is no one else but (you) to meet inside.[A place that is relatively serene and conducive to productive work. A place where you have the freedom to think and work on your dissertation.
"My Own Space" (The Act) A play by Fred Ebb

Your special space or your "kitchen" where you will be preparing your feast should have the following luxuries:

1. Proper lighting. Poor lighting increases eye fatigue. Ideal lighting is indirect and free from glare.

2. Proper ventilation. The brain needs fresh oxygen to function at its optimum.

3. Reasonable quietness. Try experimenting with soft classical or jazz music in the background, and see if that increases your concentration and productivity.

4. Proper supplies and support systems (see *Designing a Survival Kit*).

5. A DO NOT DISTURB sign. When you display this sign, it needs to be respected by those with whom you live.

1 c "E"xtend Your Note-taking and Writing Skills

Record Keeping   **Mind Mapping**   **PIE Writing**

You might find it handy to use 3" x 5" index cards to keep a **record** of references (titles of books or periodicals) you feel pertain to your research. (You should also periodically store them in a program on your computer.) You will want to be sure that you denote the author's name, relevant page numbers, any excerpts you might want to cite, and the exact page numbers of potential quotations.

You might also consider using different colors to indicate different types of references; for example, pink cards could be used for texts, green for periodicals, yellow for research reports, etc. This system will be extremely helpful to you when preparing the Research/Literature Chapter of your dissertation (see PHASE 3) and compiling your bibliography. You might also wish to create folders to store articles and references that you obtain related to your topic.

A new form of note-taking that is rapidly replacing the traditional outline form of note-taking is **mind mapping.** Some characteristics of a mind map are that it

1. stimulates the way that most people think.

2. is a means of brainstorming that allows your thoughts to flow freely.

3. helps you to categorize information and determine how this information relates to other information.

4. gives you an overview of your project.

Figure (1) is a mind map of a mind map. Carefully study the mind map for its structure, purpose, and usefulness. Notice a mind map requires only one page (preferably a blank page which is held horizontally) where related ideas are linked together. The roman numerals that are used in traditional outlining appear as branches on a mind map.

Note: Researchers claim that people who have switched from traditional outlining to mind mapping significantly increase their retention and heighten their organizational skills. In addition, mind mapping is fun, easy, and creative. Try using colored pens or pencils when creating mind maps. Experiment with each branch drawn in a different color. You might want different shades of a particular color to signify supporting ideas.

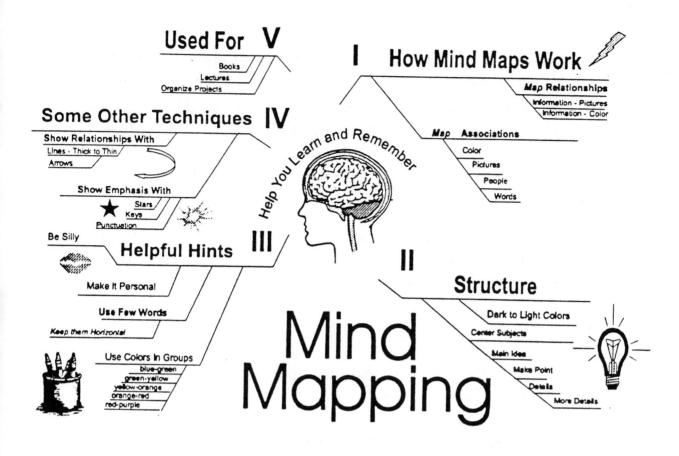

Mind Mapping

Used For V
- Books
- Lectures
- Organize Projects

I How Mind Maps Work
- Map Relationships
  - Information - Pictures
  - Information - Color
- Map Associations
  - Color
  - Pictures
  - People
  - Words

Some Other Techniques IV
- Show Relationships With
  - Lines - Thick to Thin
  - Arrows
- Show Emphasis With
  - Stars
  - Keys
  - Punctuation
- Be Silly

III Helpful Hints
- Make It Personal
- Use Few Words
- Keep them Horizontal
- Use Colors in Groups
  - blue-green
  - green-yellow
  - yellow-orange
  - orange-red
  - red-purple

Help You Learn and Remember

II Structure
- Dark to Light Colors
- Center Subjects
- Main Idea
- Make Point
- Details
- More Details

Figure 1

cutting board

Use a blank sheet of paper to create a mind map of a topic that you might want to research. Put the name of the topic in the middle of the paper. Use branches to indicate main ideas (beliefs, attitudes, and opinions) related to this topic.

To transform your notes into written passages, you might want to try a formula developed by Hanau (1975). Hanau advances the idea that written materials contain *statements* which are the declaration of beliefs, attitudes, or opinions. These *statements* are the keys which allow the reader to understand what you, the writer, are trying to convey. Each paragraph should contain a *statement* or *statements* in conjunction with supporting elements that have the function of elucidating the *statement*. These supporting elements can be classified into one of the three categories which can be remembered by the acronym **PIE**: **P**roof, **I**nformation, or **E**xamples.

1. **P**roof -- any kind of supporting documentation that a *statement* is true and/or important. In a dissertation or research paper, proof usually comes from a review of related research or a quote from a well known person or authority figure.

2. **I**nformation -- any clarifying material, such as a definition, which limits the scope of your *statements* and seeks to make clear what your *statements* mean within a certain context. This clarification brings your supporting material to bear in an effective manner.

3. **E**xample -- concrete illustrations that serve to clarify any *statement* that you make while attesting to a *statement's* truth or importance.

It is not necessary to have all three supporting elements in every paragraph of your paper, but you will probably wish to include at least two "pieces of **PIE**" per paragraph. You also need not adhere to any particular order of presenting a "statement" with its accompanying pieces of **PIE,** so long as your paragraphs are clear, sufficiently detailed, and coherent.

On the other hand, if your paragraphs are only *statements* without any pieces of **PIE,** the predominant impression that comes across is assertion without foundation. Similarly, having pieces of **PIE** without a *statement* makes it difficult for the reader to comprehend the point of what is written. Once your paragraph has a *statement* with a satisfactory helping of **PIE,** you are ready to move to the next paragraph.

cutting board:

Look at the main branches of the mind map that you created on a topic that you might wish to research. See if you can support these ideas (main branches) with the **PIE** elements described in this section.

1 c "E"nter Information into a Computer, Journal or Tape Deck

Alfieri, the great Italian dramatist allegedly had his servants tie him to his writing table so that he would be forced to write.

Hopefully, you will not need to go to the extremes that Alfieri did to discipline yourself into putting your thoughts and notes into the formation of your "feast".

Much of what makes writing difficult is trying to write and edit at the same time. Get your ideas on paper first; critique, rework, and polish them later. Critiquing ideas as you are trying to express them often represses them. If you reach a stumbling block, try to write past it -- often the best ideas lie right beyond the hurdle tempting you to give up. If you are still stuck, take a break and think over the problem in a relaxed setting. By the time you return, you will probably have the answer.

Be prepared to write at any time, in any place. Keep pen and paper in your car, purse, gym bag, pocket, etc. The best ideas often come when you are not trying for them.

If you are adept at word processing, you can save yourself a significant amount of time by transposing your notes on a regular basis onto your computer or, better yet, taking all your notes on your computer.

If you are fortunate enough to have a dedicated secretary and he/she is used to transcribing your dictation onto a word processor, that might be the ideal method for formulating your dissertation. This method of transcription offers you the liberty of creating your "feast" while in the midst of traffic.

If computers are not your "thing" and you do not have a dedicated secretary to transcribe your notes on a regular basis, perhaps you and your feast would be best served by either obtaining a wonderful pen and an ingratiating journal and proceed to WRITE; or dusting off your old faithful typewriter and preparing to TYPE. When your document is near completion, you should probably hire someone to enter your document onto a word processor so that you can make corrections and deletions and obtain an exquisite feast shortly thereafter. Be aware, however, that mastering the computer will have many benefits now (faster completion of work) and later (most organizations require a high degree of computer literacy).

cutting board:

1. What will you be using to create your feast? _____
2. When will be your first (next) time to utilize this method? _____

1 c "D"esign a Survival Kit

The following is a list of supplies and tools that you might find helpful to have in your "kitchen" while designing your "feast:"

Computer	Modem	Printer
Pencils	Pencil Sharpener	Erasers
Ruler	Graph Paper	Waste basket
Dictionary	Thesaurus	Encyclopedia
Scissors	Three hole punch	Tape
Book case	Writing table	Computer Paper
Highlighters	Colored pens	Paper clips
Calculator	Index cards	Writing paper
Clock	Comfortable chair	Surge protector

cutting board:

1. Put an asterisk (*) near the objects that you now own.

2. Put an exclamation point (!) next to the ones that you feel you should own.

3. Write down any other objects you will be needing or wanting to have in your dissertation kitchen/workspace:

_____

PICK YOUR REPAST
[Choose Your Topic]

1/2	cup	**P** ossess Knowledge of What a Dissertation Is and Is Not
1	cup	**I** dentify Your Cooking (researching) Style
1/2	cup	**C** lassify Yourself Professionally
1	cup	**K** (c) onduct the ROC Bottom Test

1/2 c "P" ossess Knowledge of What a Dissertation Is and Is Not

Before you go through the process of selecting a dissertation project and topic, it would behoove you to keep in mind that a dissertation **is not** necessarily

1. a Nobel Prize project.
2. the final answer to a pressing problem.
3. the last research paper that you will write.
4. about the "hottest" topic in your field.
5. going to excite all your friends.

What then **is** a dissertation (we hear you cry)? A dissertation is a formal research project usually required for an advanced degree which you

1. could "put your arms around." In a couple of minutes you could tell someone in your profession, as well as in another profession, what it is about.

2. already know a great deal about, and especially where it will fit into a larger picture.

3. are truly concerned and curious about.

4. could conceivably present at a professional meeting.

5. are willing to dedicate a great deal of time to complete.

6. can call your own.

7. can proclaim is a researchable, original, and contributory to your profession (see (K)conduct a ROC bottom test).

8. will know when you have completed, i.e., ascertained enough information to have accepted or not accepted your research questions or hypotheses.

1c "I" dentifying Your Style
CHOOSING YOUR RESEARCH PROJECT/TOPIC

WHAT TYPE OF COOK (RESEARCHER) ARE YOU?

Most of us have our own unique style of inquiry. Some styles embody the traditional norms of science while others exemplify non-traditional norms. There is no one right or wrong way to investigate a problem per se but if you have a very strong research style, you might find it frustrating to work on a project that is designed for a different type of researcher.

Note: It is important to keep in mind that in doing research there is room for the daring, speculative, inventive spirit who creates new theories or tries bold, imaginative experiments, as well as for the cautious, critical spirit who examines theories searchingly or for those who will patiently design experiments requiring complete attention to detail.   There are researchers who prefer the precision of mathematics and those who prefer the color of words; those who prefer to deal with human beings and human problems and others that prefer to work with computers or microscopes. However, according to Goldstein and Goldstein in their book How We Know (1985); "for all there should be the same goal- the joy and excitement of discovery and the same outcome-knowledge..."

On the cutting board that follows you will find a **"typology"** of major ways in which people make inquiries, adapted from Mitroff and Kilmann's Methodological Approaches to Social Science (1978).

Answer each question and record your answers in the spaces provided. This will give you an opportunity to discover what method or method(s) of doing research would work well for **you.**

FOR YOUR INFORMATION AND EDUCATION:
Although there are many different ways to classify types of scientific thinking, C.G. Jung's classification has been chosen because it takes into account both affect (feeling) and cognition (thinking).

cutting board:

Read each statement below, and indicate on the accompanying Likert-type scale how strongly you agree with each declaration.

1. T: *To truly understand the AIDS epidemic, one must ascertain the "truth" about AIDS. A researcher must look at the data, and make recommendations for further study based on these findings . The researcher should not base conclusions on information that is obtained through subjective means or anecdotal stories or rely too heavily on his/her personal feelings.*

disagree totally   agree totally
1   2   3   4   T = ____

2. F: *To truly understand the AIDS epidemic, one must look at the individuals who are afflicted with the disease and note the similarities and differences that exist between those tormented with AIDS. Recommendations for further study should be based on the immediate needs of those individuals as well as how the researcher feels he/she could best be personally involved.*

disagree totally   agree totally
1   2   3   4   F = ____

3. **S:** To deal with environmental problems, one should look at the methods available and determine what is the most practical way to solve these problems now, and not spend the time on some "vague" plan in the unspecified future.

disagree totally			agree totally	
1	2	3	4	S = ____

4. **I:** To deal with environmental problems, one should look at all the possibilities that exist now and, more importantly, **could** exist, and take a broad, long-range view of the situation. A quick fix to the problem should be avoided.

disagree totally			agree totally	
1	2	3	4	I = ____

To discover your research typology:

1. Enter your T,F,I, and S numbers in the spaces provided.
2. Fill in the table by computing the sums of T+I in cell I., T + S in cell II., S + F in cell III. and I + F in cell IV.
3. Your research style(s) is (are) the cell(s) with the largest sum.
4. Underline the style(s) with the largest sum.

T:_   F:_

I:_

I.	IV.
II.	III.

S:_

I. Conceptual Theorist   II. Analytical Scientist
III. Particular Humanist   IV. Conceptual Humanist

Note: If you have the luxury of selecting your own faculty advisor(s) you might want to determine what type of researcher(s) they are. Offer to conduct this test with potential advisors to see if you have compatible research styles.

What follows is a description of the archetype associated with each of the research styles above. See if the research style you have underlined suits your style of inquiry.

I. Conceptual Theorist. This type of researcher believes in TOE, i.e., *The Theory of Everything,* A conceptual theorist is holistic and imaginative. He/she believes in multiple causation's, and the development of a coherent testable framework complemented with large scale correlation. Science holds some privilege in this type of thinking, but *is not the only way that a conceptual theorist views a problem*. Motto: Conflict is an important characteristic of research and should not be dismissed. Conflict is vital to the development of both methods and theories.

II. Analytical Scientist. This type of researcher prefers *exactness, precision, and unambiguous* situations. *Science is paramount and exact in this type of thinking*. The analytical scientist sees science as ruled by nature. The ideal experiment is one where **all** the variables are controlled. Motto: In order to label something a scientific theory, it must be cast into a logical form so that given the proper antecedent conditions (X,A), one can make the valid deduction (Y). Otherwise, it is non-scientific.

III. Particular Humanist. This type of researcher prefers *personal knowledge* to *rational knowledge*. Science is not privileged in this type of thinking and is subordinate to other disciplines such as poetry and literature. The particular humanist believes that humans are too complex to study as a whole. Motto: It is absurd to think that science has remained immune to outside influences. The challenge is to develop a methodology of science that does justice not only to the humanity of the subjects studied but to the researcher as well. Only a person who is passionately involved in his/her research can make a difference.

IV. Conceptual Humanist This type of researcher prefers *holistic knowledge*. Science has no special privilege in this type of thinking. Knowledge exists only to better humanity. To further understand humanity, a conceptual humanist believes that one must study human behavior and constantly develop new theories based on these observations. Motto: The question is not "Is storytelling science?" but "Can science learn to tell a good story?"

Below are research topics that would likely appeal to the people with archetypes described above who wish to conduct an investigation of the relationship between smoking and health. Read each research topic and see if the research topic described for your archetype appeals to you.

If asked to choose a research topic on smoking and heath: Topics of Most Interest:

I. Determine the correlation between smoking and diseases, smoking and personality types, why people smoke, and as many multiple correlation's as one can ascertain between smoking and other factors.

II. Determine definitively if cigarette smoking causes cancer. Simulate smoking in laboratory animals and determine if cancer is caused.

III. Study a smoker and determine why this person started smoking and any ill effects that smoking has. Have cancer patients who have smoked keep a diary and study their feelings and concerns.

IV. Survey ex-smokers and determine the most effective ways each person was able to stop smoking

cutting board:

    1. Which of these studies appealed the most to you? _____
    2. Which appealed the least to you? _____
    3. Did you approve of the study defined for your archetype? ____ Explain: _____
    4. Keep this knowledge in mind when you select **your** dissertation topic.

1/2 c   "C" lassify Yourself Professionally

Now that you have an idea about your research style, it is important that you take this opportunity to objectively classify yourself within your profession. To choose a project that will sustain your enthusiasm, help you remain dedicated, and enable you to see to fruition in a reasonable amount of time requires a heavy dash of knowing who you are professionally and what has attracted you to your discipline.

By using a process in which you move from a broad to a narrow perspective, you will be able to discern a researchable project or projects that you are very capable of pursuing with vigor. Be aware, however, that once you are immersed in your research, you might decide to change or modify your focus. Be assured that each time you modify your study, you will be more knowledgeable and have fewer obstacles to overcome.

Use the cutting board that follows to help you formulate a dissertation topic. Dr. M. will share with you how she obtained her dissertation topic. You will be referred to as Dr.I. during this exploratory activity.(Remember to keep in mind what a *dissertation is and is not and what your research typology told you about how you like to investigate a problem.)*

cutting board:

1. What is (are) your professional role(s) or the role that you are seeking?(e.g. Are you an educator, doctor, nurse, administrator, actress, lawyer, political scientist, media person, anthropologist, engineer, computer scientist, psychologist, sociologist?)

> *Dr. M. is an educator*
> Dr. I. is _____

2. What is (are) your principal area(s) of interest(PI) or your subspecialty within your profession?

> *Dr. M. is a mathematics educator and consultant.*
> Dr. I. is _____

3. What area(s) of your PI are you most enthusiastic and/or involved with? [What made you decide to go into this profession?]

> *Dr. M. is interested and involved with mathematics anxiety, technology in the classroom, teacher training, statistics, and the future of mathematics education. She enjoys mathematics and believes that everyone could be successful in mathematics if they were given the opportunity to do math their way.*

Dr. I. is interested and involved with:

_____
_____
_____

The reasons why Dr.I. chose this profession are:

_____
_____
_____

4. What are some problems that you are interested in that you believe need some "new light," or need to be looked at critically for the first time?

> *Dr. M. believes that calculators were not being used in the elementary school classroom because of the anxiety of elementary school teachers.*

Dr. I. believes that:

_____

_____

_____

5. Restate the most pressing problem you have described using a preferred style of inquiry:

> *Dr. M. (A conceptual theorist): What is the relationship between mathematics anxiety and lack of calculator use in the classroom.*

Dr. I. _____

_____

6. Select a title (topic) based on this problem:

> *Dr. M. <u>The Wasted Resource</u>: <u>Attitudinal problems in calculator use among elementary school teachers.</u>*

Dr.: I.

**** _____

_____

Fantastic! You have yourself a research topic, Dr. I. Now, before you start your celebration, you will need to (K)conduct the ROC bottom test to see if the topic you have selected has the following attributes: **R**(esearchability), **O**(riginality), and if it is **C**(ontributory).

1c   "K" (c)onduct the ROC bottom test

> 1/3   cup   **R**   esearchability
> 1/3   cup   **O**   riginality
> 1/3   cup   **C**   ontributory

1/3 c "R" esearchability:

Use the cutting board which follows to test whether or not your topic is **researchable**. You should be able to answer "YES" to the majority of questions below.

If this is not the case then you might want to go **FISH**: **F**ind **I**nterest **S**omewhere **H**enceforth. (You would probably not want to prepare a dinner of an exotic Asian fish that you could not obtain to a group of vegetarians who would not eat this fish even if you some how manage to obtain it. Would you?)

cutting board:

    1. Are there textbooks that deal with this topic? _____
    2. Are there journals or periodicals that deal with
    this topic? _____
    3. Are there Web Sites you can visit to obtain
    information? ___
    4. Can you obtain access to files you might need? _____
    5. Can you access a sample of your population or the
    population itself? _____
    6. Will you know when you have obtained the information
    you are seeking? ___
    7. Can you obtain authorization to do your research? __
    8. Can you obtain the support of people that are
    essential to your project? ____

1/3 c "O"riginality:

A "YES" to one or more questions on the cutting board below will satisfy the "O" requirement and indicate that your topic has **originality.** If all the answers are no's, you might want to go **FISH.**

cutting board:

    1. Will this study provide some new way to look at an
    existing problem?
    2. Will this be a missing piece to an existing problem?
    3. Is this a new contradiction to an accepted point of
    view?
    4. Is this a new way to look at an historical work?
    5. Is this a recommendation from a published study?
    6. Is this a repetitive study using a different
    population or another look at a population studied
    after the passage of time?
    7. Is this a new approach to an old problem?

8. Will this be the first time a program or treatment is being evaluated in this manner?

1/3 c "C"ONTRIBUTORY:

A "YES" to at least one question on the cutting board below will satisfy the "C" requirement and indicate that your research will be **contributory**. If all the answers are no's, you might want to go **FISH**.

cutting board:

1. Is there a need in your profession to know the results of this study?
2. Will there be people in your profession or people who plan to enter this profession who will need the information that this study will ascertain?
3. Will people outside of your profession gain new insight into something in your profession after this study is complete?
4. Will some members of society, or society at large, suffer if this study was NOT done?

Once you have passed the **ROC** bottom test you will have made a major step towards obtaining your goal. Congratulations! You should feel proud and happy.

Note: A doctoral dissertation must have a very high level of quality and integrity. The entire research project and paper must be clear, lucid, logical, have an appropriate theoretical base, contain appropriate statistical analysis (if needed), and have proper citations.

Now that you have nailed down your topic, you will need to develop a solid problem statement. When this major task is accomplished, put this statement in your working environment and carry a copy of it with you whenever you are working on your dissertation. It is important never to lose sight of what you are researching and why you are conducting this research.

cutting board:

In bold print write out your research topic again in the space below:

_____

The heart of a doctoral dissertation IS the PROBLEM STATEMENT. This is the place where most assessors go first to understand and appraise the merits of your proposal or dissertation. After reading the problem statement, the reader will know *why* you are doing (did) this study and be convinced of its importance. In 250 words or less (about 1-3 paragraphs) you need to convince the reader that this study *must (had to)* be done!

The reason that you do a doctoral dissertation is because society, or one of its institutions, has some pressing problem that needs closer attention. The problem statement delineates this problem while hinting at the nature of the study-- correlation, evaluative, historical, experimental -- that is, how you will (did) solve the problem.

Once a clear and lucid problem statement is formed, all the research you put into your dissertation should be focused on obtaining a solution. You will be judged by the degree to which you find the **answer** to the problem you pose and thus achieve your purpose.

Note: A problem that results in a "yes" or "no" answer is not suitable for doctoral level research. For example, the problem: *to determine if homework is beneficial for high school students* is not appropriate for scholarly research, but the researcher can form a suitable problem statement around this topic with a bit of finesse with the statement: to *determine wherein lie the benefits of homework to high school students, if they exist.* You must say precisely what you mean in as concise a manner as possible.

A problem statement that is too narrowly focused may direct the researcher only toward trivia. A statement that is too broad may not adequately delineate the relationships or concepts involved in the study. Development of a well-constructed problem statement leads to the logical outgrowth of well constructed research questions and/or hypotheses, and supports all aspects of a research project.

Many researchers have difficulty formulating a succinct problem statement. The following activity can assist you in preparing a "delectable" problem statement. Further suggestions are offered in Phase 3.

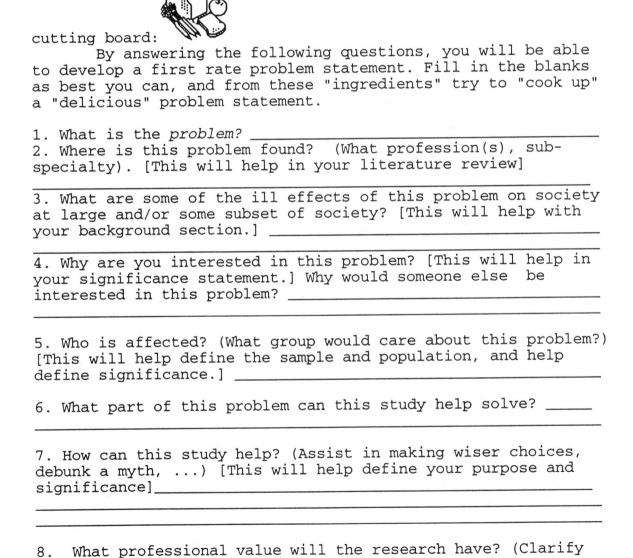

cutting board:
          By answering the following questions, you will be able to develop a first rate problem statement. Fill in the blanks as best you can, and from these "ingredients" try to "cook up" a "delicious" problem statement.

1. What is the *problem?* _____
2. Where is this problem found? (What profession(s), sub-specialty). [This will help in your literature review]
_____
3. What are some of the ill effects of this problem on society at large and/or some subset of society? [This will help with your background section.] _____
_____
4. Why are you interested in this problem? [This will help in your significance statement.] Why would someone else be interested in this problem? _____
_____

5. Who is affected? (What group would care about this problem?) [This will help define the sample and population, and help define significance.] _____

6. What part of this problem can this study help solve? _____
_____

7. How can this study help? (Assist in making wiser choices, debunk a myth, ...) [This will help define your purpose and significance]_____
_____
_____

8. What professional value will the research have? (Clarify an ambiguous point or theory, look at a new aspect of a problem, aid in an important decision-making process...) [This

helps with the purpose and significance]. What journal would
be interested in publishing this study? _____
_____

9. What needs to be done? (Analyze, describe, evaluate, test,
understand, determine...)[This will help decide the
methodology(ies) and instruments to be used] _____
_____

10. What topics, subjects, issues are involved? (stock
market, drugs, violence, language development, assessment,
euthanasia....) [This will help in the literature review] ___
_____

11. How does the study relate to the development or the
refinement of theory? _____
_____

[This will help with your theoretical framework]

12. What will result from this study? (Clarify, debunk,
relieve, assist create, recommend...) [This will help in
interpreting the results]. _____
_____

13. What harm would (could) be done if this study was NOT
done?
_____

14. optional: What has already been done about it? What hasn't
been done? Who is requesting such a study? [This will help
with your literature review].
_____
_____

**In big and bold letters, write your problem statement
in the space below. Be aware that this might be
modified a bit when you get to Phase 3.**
_____
_____
_____
_____
_____
_____
_____
_____
_____
_____
_____

Keep this with you whenever you are dissertating!

CLASSIFY YOUR REPAST--WHAT'S COOKING?

[identify your study]

The value of research is defined by how the work underway fits into the overall context of the theory or paradigm being researched. Thus, researchers must be fully cognizant of why they are doing what they are doing and what they expect the return on their efforts to be.

Gilovitch: How What We Know Isn't So (1991)

Below you will find a sampling of different types of research methodologies. This list is by no means conclusive or exhaustive but should offer you a variety of ways to classify your research. Once you have determined what type of research you will be conducting, it might be wise to find textbooks and journal articles that deal with that particular methodology in detail so that you will be aware of the intricacies of applying that methodology to your study.

One common perspective for viewing a research project is that of time. We will examine clusters of methodologies based on past, present, and future perspectives.

A
Past
Historical
Causal-Comparative
Content Analysis

B
Present
Developmental
Descriptive
Pure/Basic/Experimental
Correlational
Case Study
Phenomenological

C
Future
Action
Applied
Evaluative

D
Nouveau Cuisine:
Heuristic
Holistic
Grounded Theory
Ethnographic
Delphi

Now that you have selected your topic, you are in an excellent position to determine "what's cooking?" You are now ready to ascertain what type of a research study you will be conducting. **Research methodology** refers to the broad perspective from which you will view the problem, make the investigation, and draw inferences.

Although no single research methodology is likely to describe each aspect of the problem you are planning to investigate, there are most likely general categories into which your study will fall.

After reading the descriptions below, find the classification that best describes the nature of **your** study. We will use problems associated with low socio-economic class and its relation to education an example to show how each of these methodologies could analyze the same problem.

Use the cutting board after each example to demonstrate how the problem you are investigating *could* be resolved with each methodology.

Past Perspective

If your primary interest is in past events or factors in the past that have contributed to the problem you are researching, then your methodology will likely be historical or causal-comparative.

Historical Research: The researcher looks back at significant events in the relatively distant past and seeks, by gathering and analyzing contemporary descriptions of the event, to provide a coherent and objective picture of what happened. This reconstruction of the past is often conducted in relation to a particular theory or conceptual scheme. The data of historical research are subject to two types of evaluation: to determine if a document is authentic, or if indeed it is authentic, what the document means. The researcher is concerned with external or internal evidence and subjects the data to external or internal criticism.

Example: A study of 19th century teaching practices with children of low socio-economic class using teacher diaries as primary sources.

cutting board:

Causal-Comparative Research: The researcher looks at present characteristics of a problem, views them as the result of past causal factors and tries, by examining those past factors, to discover the causes, critical relationships, and meanings suggested by the characteristics. Usually two or more groups are compared using these characteristics.

Example: Comparison of the socio-economic status of a high-achieving group of children and a low-achieving group of children to ascertain whether and to what extent socio-economic status influences school performance.

cutting board:

Content Analysis: The researcher examines a class of social artifacts, typically written documents. Topics appropriate for content analysis include any form of communication, answering "who says what?, to whom?, why?, how,? and with what effect?" This is an unobtrusive method of doing research, but it is limited to recorded information. Coding is used to transform raw data into standardized, quantitative form. Data are analyzed through the use of official or quasi-official statistics.

Example: Documents from Title 1 programs are analyzed over a ten year period to determine any patterns or trends in entitlements.

cutting board:

Present Perspective

If your study adopts a viewpoint that is in the present time, then you will likely be examining a phenomenon as it occurs with a view to understanding its nature, organization, and/or the way it changes.

Developmental research: The researcher examines patterns and sequences of growth and change over time. This research can be done as a longitudinal study (the same group examined over a period of time) or as a cross-sectional study (different groups examined at the same time which might represent different ages or other classifications).

Example: A group of freshman students from a "high risk" school are studied to examine the factors that effect the ability to graduate in four years.

cutting board:

Descriptive Research: The researcher makes a systematic analysis and description of the facts and characteristics of a given population or event of interest. The purpose of this form of research is to provide a detailed and accurate picture of the phenomenon as a means of generating hypotheses and pinpointing areas of needed improvements.

Example: A needs assessment study of an urban ghetto is carried out as a preliminary step toward the establishment of a special pre-school program for children of low socio-economic status.

cutting board:

Correlational: The researcher investigates one or more characteristic, of a group in order to discover the extent to which the characteristics vary together. Correlational studies display the relationships among variables by such techniques as cross-tabulation and correlations.

Example: The relationship between socio-economic status and school achievement of a group of urban ghetto children is examined.

cutting board:

Pure/Basic/Experimental Research: This type of research is typically oriented toward the development of theories by discovering broad generalizations, based on careful analysis of a sample of the population being studied. It usually follows a scientific type of inquiry emphasizing a rigorous, structured analysis in each of the research stages.

When applied to the social sciences, the researcher and subjects interact in such a way that the subjects make no contribution to formulating the propositions that purport to be about them or to be based on their sayings or doings. The inquiry is all on the side of the researcher, and the action being inquired into is all on the side of the subject.

The analytical scientist's basic drive is towards certainty, that is, precision, accuracy, and reliability. In its simplest form, the experimental method attempts to control the entire research situation. The matter of control is basic to this method. The researcher seeks two matched groups, and gives one the "experimental treatment" and the other either no treatment or a placebo. Any endeavor that cannot be subjected to this type of reasoning is either suppressed, devalued, or set aside.

Example: Two groups of low socio-economic class children are randomly assigned to either an experimental enrichment program prior to entering school, or a control group of traditional pre-school play. Comparison is made of their subsequent school performances to determine whether such enrichment influences achievement.

cutting board:

Case Study: The case study method refers to descriptive research based on a real-life situation, problem, or incident; as well as cases describing situations calling for analysis, planning, decision-making, and/or action with boundaries established by the researcher. Sudzina and Kilbane (1992) maintain that the method requires that every effort be made to provide an unbiased, multidimensional perspective in presenting the case and arriving at solutions. Case study research is often used when the research questions are "how" and "why," rather than "what" and "how many." Case studies can be used when particularistic, descriptive, heuristic, and inductive phenomena are considered. The case study is dependent upon the ability to apply techniques which are multimodal to situations.

Example: A high school in a low socio-economic area is studied to gather data for an analysis of attitudes and practices as they relate to drug education.

cutting board:

Phenomenology: This type of research has its roots in existentialism. Data are structured by the subject's descriptions of the experiences and the researcher's interpretation of the descriptions. Interview is the most common instrument of data collection, which means that the quality of the data depends on the subjects' written and verbal skills. The researcher, in turn, must depend heavily on his/her intuitive skills. It is usually wise for the researcher to frame his/her own feelings, attitudes, biases, and understandings of the phenomenon prior to conducting a phenomenological study.

Example: A researcher spends several months at an inner-city high school to determine the perceptions of the teachers and students with respect to school policies.

cutting board:

Future Perspective

If your prime interest is, in studying a current situation for the purpose of contributing to a decision about it, changing it, or establishing a policy about it, you will probably use one of the following future-oriented research methodologies:

Applied or Evaluative Research: This type of research is concerned primarily with the application of new knowledge for the solution of day-to-day problems. The knowledge obtained is thus contextual. Its purpose is to improve a process by testing theoretical constructs in actual situations. In medical research a cardiologist might monitor a group of heart disease patients to see if the diet prescribed by the American Heart Association is truly effective. A great deal of social research fits into this category, for it attempts to establish whether various organizations and institutions are fulfilling their purpose. The relationship between researcher and subject is one of expert and client.

Many social action programs have been researched in this manner. It highlights the symbols of measurement and scientific neutrality but attempts to minimize the influence of the behavioral science perspective.

Example: An income-enhanced program for raising the socio-economic status of parents of pre-school children is evaluated for its effects upon school performance of children.

cutting board:

Action Research   This is a type of applied research which is more concerned with immediate application than with the development of a theory. It focuses on specific problems in a particular situation and usually involves those who can immediately create change. Bogdan and Biklen (1992) describe action research as a systematic collection of information that is designed to bring about social change. This kind of research allows that there could be more than one right way to develop solutions to problems.

The beginnings of "action research" date back to Lewin (1946). In his study of "group decision and social change," he used his model to describe how to change people's relationship to food. His research consisted of analysis, fact-finding, conceptualization, planning, execution, more fact-finding, conceptualization, etc. Marrow (1969) saw the Lewin model as a means of studying subjects through changing them and seeing the effect. This type of inquiry is based on the belief that in order to gain insight into a process one must introduce a change and then observe its variable effects and new dynamics.

Example: A program in which teachers are given in-service workshops and new materials to use with low socio-economic status children is implemented in two pilot schools, evaluated as it progresses, and continually modified to become more effective.

cutting board:

"Nouveau Cuisine"

Below is a list of some non-traditional meals that have been successfully served at modern day banquets.

Heuristic Research: In "action research," hypotheses are being created and tested whereas in heuristic research, the investigator encourages individuals to discover their own hypotheses in relation to a problem and decide on methods which would enable them to investigate further on their own.

In "heuristic research" the emphasis is on personal commitment rather than linear methodologies. Its purpose is to describe a meaningful pattern as it exists in the universe without any pre-designed plan, thus eliminating suggestive speculation This type of research intrinsically tends to be more open ended than most.

FOR YOUR INFORMATION AND EDUCATION:

Clark Moustakas (1961) did a study on loneliness based on his own personal experiences and after its publication, several "lonely" people picked up on his work and furthered the study. He then published their studies so that others could gain more insight into this situation.

> Moustakas felt this type of "heuristic research" recognizes the significance of inner searching's for deeper awareness. He saw this approach as an integration of searching, studying, an as an openness to new experiences, intuition, and process. Critics of "heuristic research" feel that it is just an elaboration of the problem stage of research and should not be construed as the research itself.

Example: An adult from a low socio-economic class obtains a Ph.D., and seeks out other such people, to ask them a series of questions, in order to point out the similarities and differences in their responses.

cutting board:

Holistic Research: In "holistic research," qualities of traditional research, such as a systematic inquiry and rigorous search for the truth, are given the same priority as relevancy, intuition, and human dignity.

While traditional research relies almost exclusively on references to previously peer-reviewed studies, holistic research often gives details of political standpoints, current works, and relationships from a variety of sources. Generally, you would choose this type of research methodology if you feel a need for exploring **all** methods of inquiry including the use of fictional literature, art, and music where applicable, or if you are attempting to create a new theory or identify a new problem.

Holistic researchers feel that the tendency of traditional researchers to rely heavily on test results and to over specialize is a serious shortcoming which trivializes people and shows little humility. Maslow (1970) has stated that "if you prod at people like things they won't let you know them."

Holistic theories tend to be concatenated rather than hierarchical and are loosely linked to the whole.

Example: Two pre-school children, one from a low socio-economic family and the other from a high socio-economic family, are studied to determine the patterns of educational development in each. Their artwork, play activities, interaction with peers, etc. are used to help the researcher make inferences about their cognitive, conative, and affective development.

Grounded Theory: This type of inquiry, also known as "analytic induction," is one of the most sophisticated and developed approaches to rigorous qualitative (non-numerical) research. This type of research has its roots in symbolic interactionism and philosophy, and is used in areas where there is little previous research or in familiar areas where a new viewpoint would be greatly valued. Each piece of datum is compared to every other piece of datum as it is collected. Data are usually collected by participant observation and formal semi-structured interview. Data are simultaneously being collected, organized, analyzed, and interpreted to form new theories.

In "grounded theory" the researcher decides what data to collect next on the basis of an "emerging" theory. Proponents of grounded theory [see Glaser and Strauss (1967)], believe that conjecture must be generated from data by a constant comparison method, that is, a series of "double back steps" until a pattern finally emerges.

Example: Pre-school children from low socio-economic families are interviewed to determine their concerns regarding education. Once this information is collected, the researcher explores the areas delineated with similar groups of children to determine the extent of these concerns.

cutting board:

_____

Ethnographic: This type of study has its roots in anthropology and seeks to develop an understanding of the cultural meanings people use to organize and interpret their experiences. This can be done through an "emic" approach (studying behaviors from within a culture) or through an "etic" approach (studying behaviors from outside the culture and examining similarities and differences across cultures). Data are usually obtained through participant observation by the researcher or research assistant and then verified with the group living the phenomenon.

Example: High school students from low socio-economic families videotape different types of educational institutions that they have attended, and determine, from their perspective, the most pressing problems within these institutions. They then make recommendations as to how these problems might best be remedied.

cutting board:

_____

Delphi research technique: This involves a series of questionnaires, each more structured and requiring more focus by the respondent than the preceding one. Delphi technique is used when the problem does not lend itself to precise analytical techniques, but can benefit from subjective judgments on a collective basis.

Delphi is primarily used in two modes: exploratory (to find out what's "out there"); and refinement (using "expert judgments" anonymously elicited to fine-tune quantitatively-oriented estimates). For the technique to work, the respondents' estimates need to be calibrated for over/under estimation errors; the questions need to be neutrally-phrased; and some technique or researcher oversight is necessary to control for the inclusion of mutually exclusive data components in the Delphi analysis. This technique is gaining more popularity as members of listservs feed back information and perhaps try to come to a consensus on future directives.

Example: A researcher directs identical questions to a group of experts, asking them to give their opinions on how to educate children from low socio-economic areas. In the next step, the researcher makes a summary of all the replies s/he has received, sends this to the respondents and asks if any expert wants to revise his/her original response.

cutting board:

_____

FOR YOUR INFORMATION AND EDUCATION:

Research methodologies can also be placed into two categories: quantitative or qualitative. Although there is no rigid demarcation between qualitative and quantitative methods, there are some salient differences between these two major epistemologies [besides the obvious "L" in the former and "N" in the latter :)].

In general, qualitative methodologies favor the view that the world is holistic, and that there is no single reality. Such methods further support the view that reality, which is based on perceptions, is different for each person, changes over time, and derives meaning primarily from context. Below find some differences between qualitative and quantitative epistemologies.

QUALITATIVE	QUANTITATIVE
Theory Development	Theory Testing
Naturalistic or Organic Settings	Synthetic Settings
Subjective	Objective
Observations, interviews, descriptive statistics	Tests, Surveys inferential statistics
Generates hypothetical propositions	Generates predictive relationships

And the winner is...
    Which research methodology best describes the way *you plan to* do your study? Why?

_____

_____

    Which methodology was the runner up? Why?

_____

_____

Terrific! You have just taken another important step towards successfully completing your dissertation. Keep cooking! In the next cutting board you can demonstrate your scholarly literacy by matching the research term with its description. Check your answers and make sure you master the nuances of the ones that you missed.

cutting board:

A TEST OF YOUR RESEARCH ACUMEN

1. hermeneutics

A) A theory in the field of criticism in which all texts and works of art have a multiplicity of meanings.

2. postmodern

B) A philosophical movement founded by Edmund Husset based on the relationship between a subject and the objects in his/her world.

3. ontology

C) The art and craft of interpretation which concerns itself with secret and hidden meanings in texts, music, and works of art.

4. phenomenology

D) Concerned with the nature of knowledge. In particular the methodology used to derive, elicit, and analyze data.

5. historical

E) A test, survey, or questionnaire used for data collection.

6. epistemology

F) A strong dislike of particular persons, groups or things. An attitude that does not require action or an elaborate rationale.

7. qualitative

G) A philosophical view of seeking to understand what reality is or what reality consists of.

8. deconstruction

H) A study centered on culture. The purpose is to develop an understanding of the cultural meanings people use to organize and interpret their experiences.

9. case study

I) A type of study based on feedback with the hope of coming to some type of consensus.

10. ethnographic

J) A movement that suggests multiple interpretations of events and that all knowledge is subjective.

11. delphi

K) A set of interrelated constructs, definitions, and propositions that presents a systematic view of phenomena.

12. theory

L) Research focused on reliable and replicable data, mostly deductive in nature. Assumes that attributes can be expressed in measurable terms. Objective.

13. bias

M) Research focused on inductive discovery, tends to be exploratory, descriptive, process oriented, and concerned with theory development.

14. instrument

N) A research method that aims to assess the meaning of events and to interpret what might otherwise be considered merely as the happenstance of blind fortune.

15. quantitative

O) An intensive description and analysis of a particular social unit that seeks to uncover the interplay of significant factors that are characteristic of a unit.

Ans: 1-C, 2-J, 3-G, 4-B, 5-N, 6-D, 7-M, 8-A, 9-O, 10-H. 11-I, 12- K, 13-F, 14-E, 15-L

BE AWARE OF HEALTH HAZARDS
[Ethics of Research]

1 cup	RESPONSIBILITY
1 cup	COMPETENCE,
1 cup	MORAL AND LEGAL ISSUES
1 cup	PROPER REPRESENTATION

Now that you have selected a research topic and have placed it into a particular category, you are in an excellent position to digest research **ethics.**

The dictionary defines ethics as "moral principles or rules of conduct." Morals are defined as "that concerning right and wrong." Research ethics are, therefore, the rules of right and wrong concerning research. Since research almost always involves people it is important that your research does not affect people in a negative way.

Research inherently contains many paradoxes. As a researcher you need freedom to investigate, that is to find out as much information as possible about the population you are studying, while adhering to an individual's "right to privacy." Ethical principles have been established to balance these issues.

1 c RESPONSIBILITY

"The researcher must have a fantastic love of truth."
Flaws and Fallacies in Statistical Thinking ...
Stephen Campbell

It is the responsibility of the researcher to have integrity, that is, truthfulness and honesty when carrying out the project. Deliberately changing or inventing research results to suit your own ideas is anathema in research.

In traditional scientific research **objectivity** is the key word. Traditional research is based on facts and figures, not on personal opinions and **biases.** The researcher is not to affect or influence the subjects' opinions.

It is important, regardless of the type of research you are doing, that you respect the culture and customs of the people you are studying and be rid of any cultural biases when carrying out and reporting research.

FOR YOUR INFORMATION AND EDUCATION:

The following is a resumé of the Code of Ethics of the American Sociological Association.

1. Researchers must maintain scientific objectivity.
2. Researchers must recognize the limitations of their competence and not attempt to engage in research beyond such competence.
3. Every person is entitled to the right of privacy and dignity of treatment.
4. All research should avoid causing personal harm to subjects used in research.
5. Confidential information provided by a research subject must be held in strict confidentiality by the researcher.
6. Research findings should be presented honestly, without distortion.

7. The research must not use the prerogative of a researcher to obtain information for other than professional purposes.
8. The researcher must acknowledge all assistance, collaboration of others, or sources from which information was borrowed.
9. The researcher must acknowledge financial support in the research report or any personal relationship of the researcher with the sponsor that may conceivably affect the research findings.
10. The researcher must not accept any favors, grants, or other means of assistance that would violate any of the ethical principles set forth above.

"Statistics are like bikinis. What they reveal is suggestive, but what they conceal is vital."

Aaron Levenstein

You have an obligation, as a researcher, to use statistics responsibly. An awareness of statistical fallacies and deceptions can serve as a guide for "what not to do" in reporting information and help you become a more critical reviewer of other research that you study. Some common statistical fallacies to be aware of are:

Spurious accuracy - The story is told about a man who when asked the age of a certain river replied that it was 3,000,004 years old. When asked how he arrived at this conclusion he claimed that when he first started coming to this river he was told it was 3,000,000 years old and that was exactly four years ago.

This is an example of spurious accuracy. Many things can simply not be measured with as much accuracy as some purveyors wish to pretend.

Faulty comparisons - In 1960 commercials for Hollywood Bread claimed it had fewer calories per slice than any other bread. The FTC maintained that the only reason a slice of Hollywood bread contained fewer calories was that is was more thinly sliced. The comparison was based on unequal units. Whenever two or more things are being compared with respect to one characteristic, it is necessary that important characteristics (dependent variables) are kept as similar as possible. [It is unethical that while comparing apples and oranges the reader is given the impression that what is being compared are two apples].

Accommodating averages- There are many kinds of averages. From a formal statistical standpoint, some are more common then others. The average that most people relate to is the (arithmetic) **mean** average which is a measure of central tendency obtained by adding all entries and dividing by the number of entries.

The **median** average is the number in the middle when all the entries are listed in chronological order (if there are an even number of entries, then the median is the arithmetic mean of the middle two, the $n/2$ entry and the $n/2 +1$ entry). The median is easy to compute, and takes into account all the data, but is not sensitive to the magnitude of the data. (For example, it doesn't care if the last number was 0 or -34.)

The **mode** average is the term that occurs the most often. Although it is usually the easiest figure to obtain, it is sensitive only to the most common occurrence and thus does not take into consideration all the numbers.

Less frequently used "averages" are the **harmonic mean** (used to average different rates, e.g. if you traveled at 50 mph for 2 hours and 60 mph for 3 hours then you would have traveled a total of 280 miles in 5 hours at an average of 56 miles for the entire trip), and the **geometric mean** (used to average rates of growth).

A manager of a baseball team might find the median or mode average more advantageous than the mean average when negotiating salaries with players. The players, on the other hand may prefer to use the arithmetic mean salary so that the salaries of the players who are making *astronomical* amounts would be considered and weighted into the determination of their wages.

The arithmetic mean average, although it is sensitive to all the data, does not, by itself, give us a picture of how the data is dispersed. To accomplish this the **standard deviation** or the **variance**, which is the standard deviation squared, should be reported. The variance is found by taking the difference between each entry and the mean, squaring these differences, and obtaining the (arithmetic) mean of the squared differences. To obtain the standard deviation all you, or your calculator, need do is take the square root of the variance.

If the standard deviation is relatively large compared to the mean, a wide dispersion of numbers is indicated. Conversely, a small standard deviation indicates that the numbers are clustered around the mean. Thus, it is generally expected that the researcher report the mean and standard deviation when presenting his/her findings.

The following is an empirical rule that applies to data having a distribution that is approximately bell shaped:

- about 68% of all scores fall within one standard deviation of the mean.
- about 95% of all scores fall within two standard deviations of the mean.
- about 99% of all scores fall within three standard deviations of the mean.

e.g. The mean IQ. on the Stanford-Binet Test is 100 and the standard deviation is 15. Thus, 68% of those who have taken the test have I.Q.'s between 85 and 115. This is often referred to as "normal." I.Q.'s between 115 and 130 are considered "above average," those with I.Q.'s between 130 and 145 are considered "genius," and those above 145 are classified as "brilliant."

Ad hoc definitions- Whenever a term can be defined in more than one way, you must decide which of the possible definitions seems most sensible and which definition lends itself best to efficient data collection. [It is also important that you clearly define all concepts in your study which might be unfamiliar to your reader.]

A classic case of the need for a proper definition was found in 1955 when the population of London was reported in three different studies as:

5,200   325,000   8,315,000

whereas New York City was reported (in three different studies) to have a population of:

1,910,000   10,350,000   8,050,000

What became clear from these accounts is how meaningless a comparison between the populations of these cities (or any city) is without clearly defining geographic boundaries.

Rubber graphs --The human eye has difficulty assimilating raw data or columns of numbers. Graphs often aid in making information more easily understood. A line graph is customarily used to note trends or compare amounts. The vertical axis generally has the measures (quantities) represented. The scales that are used will affect the appearance of the graph and should not be used to deceive people.

The murky notion of cause and effect --The story is told about a man who wrote a letter to an airline requesting that their pilots cease turning on the little light that says "FASTEN SEAT BELTS," because every time that light went on, the ride got bumpy. Be aware that in all correlational studies, effects may be wrongly attributed to factors that were merely "casually" associated rather than cause-and effect related.

1c COMPETENCE

You should be properly qualified to carry out your research project. You should look at the problem you plan to study critically, then objectively as possible judge your own abilities to devise procedures appropriate for examining the problem.

A competent researcher possesses certain personal qualities such as creativity, flexibility, curiosity, determination, objectivity, tolerance of frustration, logical reasoning abilities, and the ability to make scholarly observations. [Having come this far in your Dissertation Cookbook, you have already demonstrated many of these qualities.]

1c MORAL AND LEGAL ISSUES

The legal and social rules of the community you are investigating should be respected. If you think your work could break either the legal or social rules of the community, your research efforts should be curtailed until these issues are resolved.

Subjects often need to be assured that all personal information given to the researcher will be seen only by those who are carrying out the research project. It is unethical to discuss a person or the information he or she gives you even in confidence with your family or friends. There is one exception to the confidentiality rule -- legal obligation. If someone tells you about a serious legal offense or crime, you may have to break the confidentiality rule and notify the proper authorities.

Most research reports on groups of people keep the identity of individuals anonymous. When reporting anecdotal cases, identities can be hidden by the use of a false name or initials.

When you interview or test people you should explain to them the following:

1. Who will see the information they give;

2. What will be done with the information; and

3. How their privacy will be protected.

It is important for you, the researcher, to be viewed as a person concerned about the people being studied. You should not leave confidential questionnaires, papers or interview notes lying around so that anyone can read them. It is best to keep these somewhere safe or, if possible, locked away so that they don't fall into the wrong hands.

1c PROPER REPRESENTATION

Misrepresentation is unacceptable. When you carry out research you may find you have a powerful position and high status. You should not claim to have more qualifications than you actually have.

Researchers are responsible for protecting the welfare and dignity of the people they are researching. You must have informed consent from all subjects taking part in the research. If people do not want to continue, they must have the right to withdraw without any repercussions.

In human research it is unethical (and often impossible) to arrange for negative conditions such as poor teaching, abusive parenting, alcoholism, etc.; however, the consequences of such conditions can be studied.

WARNING: In this age of information, sponsored studies have become America's most powerful and popular tool of persuasion. Although such studies and surveys wear the guise of objective science, their findings almost invariably reflect their sponsors' intentions. Most such research is designed with a certain outcome in mind, and it is all but guaranteed to achieve that outcome. The result is a corruption of information-- the information used every day by voters, consumers, and leaders. "Studies have become the vehicle for polishing corporate images, influencing juries, shaping debate on public policy, selling commercial products and satisfying the media's -- and the public's-- voracious appetite for information." In The Tainted Truth (1995), Cynthia Crossen details popular studies which succinctly illustrate this grave situation.

What can be done?

It is idealistic to believe that academic institutions, researchers, pollsters or the media will universally decide to stifle their self-interest and clean up the information industry. One of the unfortunate results of our obsession with numbers and information is that we allow them to supersede our eyes, our judgment, and our common sense. Many people are afraid to try to pull apart statistics because they were "not good in math." What follows are things to think about while evaluating the veracity of OPR (other people's research):

1. A little skepticism goes a long way: Does this make sense? Does it seem right?

2. Unless and until a study has been replicated, it should be looked at with care.

3. Beware of "independent" researchers. This means they have many paying clients instead of one.

4. Beware of "nonprofit" researchers. They still count on a regular salary.

5. Beware of phrases like "as many as." This indicates hyperbole.

6. What kind of reputation does the researcher enjoy as a supplier of the information or as an authority on the subject?

7. Does the investigator have an "ax to grind?"

8. What supportive evidence is offered?

9. Some basic questions:

    a) How many people were involved?

    b) Over what period of time?

    c) How was the study controlled for bias?

    d) What did earlier studies find?

    e) How were results presented?

    f) Was the research peer-reviewed?

    g) What kind of reputation does the source enjoy as a supplier of this type of information?

    h) Is the source an authority on the subject?

    i) What supportive evidence is offered?

    j) Do estimates appear plausible?

Ultimately, the job of cleaning up the research business is everyone's responsibility.

CHOOSE YOUR ATTIRE
(Form and Style)

When you attend a formal dinner, you are often advised on what the dress code will be: white tie, black tie, casual attire, etc. The same can be said for the serving or presenting of your feast (final dissertation copy): A certain **form and style** should be adhered to.

Assembling the final manuscript of your dissertation usually requires adherence to a certain form and style with respect to each of the following aspects:

Pagination,   footnotes,   abbreviations,   tables, illustrations,   bibliography,   references, quotations,   layouts,   capitalization,   underlining,

graphs, indenting, table of contents, acknowledgments, title page, chapter headings, parentheses, spacing, table of tables, page numbering, punctuation marks, hyphenations

Shortly after you start writing the preliminary draft of your research paper, it would be an excellent idea for you to determine what will be the format of your paper. The most important rule to follow is that of consistency, i.e., once you have determined that you will be using a certain style and form of writing, continue to use *that* exact style and form throughout your manuscript.

You should obtain a manual that aids writers in your discipline with respect to form and style. Such manuals do exist for the biological sciences, engineering, humanities, law, mathematics, physical science, and psychology. It would also be helpful for you to scrutinize an approved dissertation from a colleague or classmate in your field with respect to the form and style they used or examine a dissertation in your field that is currently living in a university library.

The American Psychological Association (APA) manual is the most common style and form guide used by researchers in the social and behavioral sciences. Below are some examples of how to reference books used as references in your research document according to APA guidelines.

One Author: Nathan, A.J. (1990). China's crisis: Dilemmas of reform and prospects for democracy. New York: Columbia University Press.

Two authors: Simon, M., & Francis, B. (1997). The dissertation cookbook. Dubuque, IA: Kendall Hunt.

Three authors: Linn, M., Fabricant, S., & Linn, D. (1988). Healing the eight stages of life. New York: Paulist Press.

More than three authors: Sakakibara, S., Hidetoshi, Y., Hisakatsu, S.,Kengo, S., & Shimon, F. (1988). The Japanese stockmarket: Pricing system. New York: Praeger.

   No author: Diseases. (1983). Springhouse, PA: Nursing 84 Books.

   Corporate author: American Hospital Association. (1988). American hospital association guide to the health care field. Chicago: Author.

   Editor: Adams, M. (Ed.). (1987). The Middle East handbook. New York: Facts on File.

PHASE 2

```
┌─────────────────────────────────────────┐
│  ACCOUTREMENTS                            │
│  Utensils                                 │
│  [Instruments]                            │
│  Assistant Chefs                          │
│  [Population and Sample]                  │
│  Serving Platters/Spices                  │
│  [Statistics]                             │
└─────────────────────────────────────────┘
```

Utensils:
[choosing your instruments]

What will you utilize to gather data?

Tests, Inventories, Questionnaires, Interviews, Observations

In PHASE 2 of the Dissertation Cookbook you will acquire proper utensils for the creation and serving of your feast. In addition, during this phase you will be forming the "bulk" of your main course which you will ultimately complete in PHASE 3.

Pre-Packaged Tests and Inventories
(Just Stir and Serve)

Pre-Packaged **tests and inventories** are among the most useful tools for the chef/researcher. They have been seen at many eloquent banquets in the past. The benefits of using pre-packaged and standardized tests are that the items and total scores have been carefully analyzed and their validity and reliability have most likely been established by careful statistical controls.

Most pre-packaged tests have norms that are based upon the performance of many subjects of various ages living in many different types of communities and geographic areas. Among those to choose from are:

1. **Achievement tests,** which attempt to measure what an individual has learned. Achievement tests are designed to quantify an individual's level of performance based on information that has been deliberately taught. Most tests used in schools are achievement tests. They are used to determine individual or group status in academic learning; strengths and weaknesses defined by the test preparer; and as a basis for awarding prizes, scholarships, or degrees.

2. **Aptitude tests,** which attempt to predict the degree of achievement that may be expected from individuals in a particular activity. They are similar to achievement tests in their measuring of past learning, but differ in their attempt to measure non-deliberate or unplanned learning. They are often used to divide students into relatively homogeneous groups for instructional purposes, identify students for scholarship grants, screen for educational programs, and purportedly to predict future successes.

FOR YOUR INFORMATION AND EDUCATION:

The case has been made that most achievement and aptitude tests do not accurately predict academic achievement. Many people feel that the questions and concepts being tested are culturally biased. Efforts are being made to develop culture-free tests that eliminate this undesirable quality, but such tests have yet to meet universal approval.

3. **Personality tests or inventories** are used by subjects to report their own personality traits, or tendencies. However, because of many peoples inability or unwillingness to report their own actions accurately and objectively, their tendency to withhold embarrassing responses, and their unwillingness to express those qualities that are socially unacceptable, the effectiveness and the value of such tests are limited.

4. **Psychological tests and inventories** are instruments designed to describe and measure certain aspects of human behavior.

To determine if a pre-packaged test would be right for you, it would be an excellent idea to do an in-depth analysis of each question on each test that purports to measure a **variable** (characteristic) that you are examining. It is your responsibility to provide evidence that the examination selected is the most appropriate for the purpose at hand.

FOR YOUR INFORMATION AND EDUCATION:

One of the best sources to help you select standardized tests are the Mental Measurements Yearbooks, edited by Oscar Buros and published by Gryphon Press. These yearbooks contain critical evaluations of tests and provide information concerning costs, availability of alternate forms, administration time required, names of subtests, grade or age levels for which the tests were designed, and the name of publisher. It is, however, necessary to know the approximate year in which the exam was published to determine in which yearbook any particular exam was reviewed.

cutting board:

1. If you are planning to use a pre-packaged test or survey, write the name of the test and its reliability and validity information in the space below:

_____
_____
_____

2. List the questions that you feel this test will answer with respect to some variable or characteristic you wish to measure in your study.

_____
_____
_____

Questionnaires
(Making your meal from scratch)

Questionnaires are perhaps the most frequently used instrument for gathering data on population variables. Their appeal rests in their ability to get to the heart of the research under investigation.

The questionnaire often attempts to gather background characteristics such as age, education, gender, etc., and to elicit the feelings, beliefs, experiences, or activities of the respondents. It is used to help policy makers, program planners, evaluators, and researchers when information needs to come directly from the people.

Good questionnaires maximize the relationship between the answers recorded and the variable that the researcher is trying to measure. The answer is valuable to the extent that it can be shown to have a predictable relationship to facts or subjective states that are of interest.

One means of assuring that the questions are germane to the study is for the researcher to prepare a working table containing a list of questions related to the hypothesis under investigation. You will be given that opportunity in the cutting board activity provided in this section.

A consideration that needs to be made is what type of data will you obtain. There are four types of data that you can obtain. A mnemonic device used to remember these types of data is found in the French word for black, **NOIR (nominal, ordinal, interval, ratio)**: nominal and ordinal data are considered **non-parametric** data (non-numerical), whereas interval and ratio are considered **parametric** (numerical) data.

1. **N**ominal (name only) data are characterized by information that consist of names, labels, or categories only. This type of data cannot be arranged in an ordering scheme and is considered to be the lowest level of measurement. There is no criterion by which values can be identified as greater than or less than other values. We cannot, for example, average 12 democrats and 15 republicans and come up with 13.5 independents. We can, however, determine ratios and percentages and compare the results to other groups.

2. **O**rdinal (or ranked) levels of measurement generate data that may be arranged in some order, but differences between data values either cannot be determined or are meaningless. For example, we can classify income as: low, middle, or high to provide information about relative comparisons, but the degrees of differences are not available.

3. **Interval** levels of measurement are similar to the ordinal level, with the additional property that you can determine meaningful amounts of difference between data. This level, however, often lacks an inherent starting point. For example, in comparing the annual mean temperatures of states the value of "0 degrees" does not indicate no heat, and it would be incorrect to say that 40 degrees is half as warm as 80 degrees.

4. **R**atio levels of measurement are considered the highest level of measurement. They include an inherent zero starting point and fractional values. As the name implies, ratios are meaningful for this type of measurement. The heights of children, distances traveled, and the amount of gasoline consumed, are ratio levels of measurement.

A general and important guideline to follow is that *statistics based upon one level of measurement should not be used for a lower level.* Implications made from interval and rational data can usually be determined by using **parametric methods**, whereas implications from ordinal and nominal data require the use of less sensitive **nonparametric methods**.

Another decision that you need to make is whether to use open-ended questions or close-ended questions.

The advantages of open questions are:

1. You will be able to obtain answers that were unanticipated;

2. They tend to describe more closely the real views of the respondent; and

3. Respondents will be able to answer questions in their own words.

However, closed questions are usually an easier way of creating data because:

1. The respondent can perform more reliably the task of answering the question when response alternatives are given;

2. The researcher can perform more reliably

the task of interpreting the meaning of answers when the alternatives are given to the respondent;

3.   Providing respondents with a constrained number of categories increases the likelihood that there will be enough people in any given category to be analytically interesting; and

4.   There is a strong belief that respondents find closed questions to be less threatening than open questions.

cutting board:

If you are planning to create a questionnaire, fill out the information below:

1.   List four demographic questions you feel would be helpful to know about your sample:

_____
_____
_____
_____

2.   What questions are you seeking answers to in your study?

_____
_____
_____

3.   List four other broad questions that you would like to obtain from your sample?

_____
_____
_____
_____

4.   Underline the type of measurements you will most likely use:
        Nominal (name only, certain trait),
        Ordinal (a ranking system; Likert scale),
        Interval (fixed differences, but no fixed zero;
            temperature)

Ratio (interval with a fixed zero; height, time, weight)

5. Underline the type of questions you will most likely be asking.

Open (subjects fill in the blanks)
Closed (multiple choice)

6. What is the population you are studying?
_____

7. Will you be sending the questionnaire to the whole population or to a subset of the population (sample)? _____

8. Will the survey be administered **cross-sectional**? (just once) or **longitudinal**? (over time)
_____

9. How will the survey be administered? Through the mail? Personal interview? In a group setting?
_____

10. Approximately how many questions do you plan to have? _____

11. Will you need permission and/or help to administer the questionnaire or obtain a mailing list? ____ If yes, how will you obtain this assistance?
_____

The following suggestions can help you eliminate some obstacles that questionnaire designers often encounter. As you prepare your questions, check to see that each adheres to the warnings given.

____1. When writing closed-ended questions, it is an excellent idea to use standard English.

____2. Keep the questions concrete and close to the respondents' experience.

____3. Be aware of words, names, and views that might automatically bias results.

___4.	Use a single thought per question.

___5.	Use short questions and ask for short responses if possible.

___6.	Avoid words that may be unfamiliar to the respondent.

___7.	Define any word whose meaning might be vague.

___8.	Avoid questions with double negatives, such as: "This class is not the worst math class I have ever taken."

___9. When using multiple choice questions, make sure all possibilities are covered.

___10.	Be as specific as possible.

___11.	Avoid questions with two or more parts.

___12.	Give points of reference as comparisons, e.g.,

Instead of asking, "Do you like Mathematics?" you might ask:

Please rank your favorite academic class from most favorite (1), to least favorite (4):
Social studies _____ English _____ Science _____ Mathematics____

___13. <u>Underline</u> or use **bold** print for words that are critical to the meaning of the questions, especially negative words like **<u>not.</u>**

___14.	Ask only important questions since most respondents dislike long questionnaires or questionnaires that ask too many unimportant questions.

___15.	Avoid suggestive questions or questions that contain biases, e.g.,

"Would you support more money in mathematics education if the schools continue to use the same out dated teaching methods?"

Such a question reflects the writers bias on mathematics education.

___16. When asking questions regarding ethnic background or political affiliations, it is a good idea to use alphabetical order.

In addition the following receive high honors in the culinary research arts:

___17. Efficiency and brevity -- the questionnaire should only be as long as necessary.

___18. Objectivity -- the test should be as objective as the situation dictates.

___19. Interesting-- the questionnaire should be as interesting and as enjoyable as possible.

___20. Simplicity -- the questionnaire should be simple to administer, score, and interpret.

___21. Clarity -- it is important that the directions be clear so that each participant can understand exactly the manner in which the questionnaire is to be answered.

A widely used type of ordinal measurement used on closed questionnaires is the **Likert-type** scale, named after its creator. The original Likert scale used five categories: strongly approve, approve, undecided, disapprove, strongly disapprove.

In a Likert-type scale, points are assigned to each of the categories being used. The most favorable response is usually given the most points, that is, favorableness of the attitude, not the response category itself. A Likert-type scale may use fewer or more than five categories. In general, the more categories there are, the better the reliability. The placement of items should be randomized. Placing all of the favorably worded items first may produce a set or tendency for respondents. (e.g. ,The subjects might fill in all (5's) without reading the questions).

The score that the individual receives on a Likert-type scale is the sum of the scores received on each item. For example, if 25 items are on a questionnaire and each item contains a minimum of (1) point and a maximum of (5) points, then the highest possible score would be 125, whereas, the lowest possible score would be 25 (assuming no items were missing).

FOR YOUR INFORMATION AND EDUCATION:

One approach to elicit more reflective thinking from the respondent is to list general questions first, followed by more specific ones. If the inquiry has controversial aspects such as sexual behavior, then it would be wise to begin with the least threatening questions such as the respondent's birthplace, gender, health, occupation, etc., and then gradually lead into the more contentious questions.

Once you have custom designed your questionnaire or test, you will need to consider the instrument's reliability and validity.

Reliability provides an estimate of how well measurements reflect true (non random) differences.

There are three main types of reliability coefficients that can be measured:

•**stability**-- the extent to which individuals maintain their relative standings when the same or similar exam is administered twice over a period of time.

•**equivalence**-- correlation of scores on two or more forms of the same test by the same persons.

•**internal consistency**-- correlation between questions on the same test to determine if they measure the same trait.

As a researcher, you are obligated to select the most reliable instruments. The purpose of the testing determines, in part, the minimum reliability coefficient that can be tolerated. However, reliable tests may not necessarily be valid tests.

Validity refers to the extent to which measurements achieve the purpose for which they are designed. The researcher needs to determine the validity of the content.

Some questions that could determine whether or not a test is valid are:

1. Does each item measure predetermined criteria?

2. Do previously obtained scores accurately predict the criteria measured?

3. Do the behaviors or conditions of administrating the test affect the results?

cutting board:

This would be an excellent time to create your questionnaire. Insert a separate sheet of paper and compose your questionnaire now! Check to see that you have incorporated the ideas suggested in this section. Enjoy the challenge!

Adjuncts to Questionnaires
Pilot Study
Cover Letter
Going the Extra Mile

Pilot Study

Before the final form of the questionnaire is constructed, it is useful to conduct a **pilot study** to determine if the items are yielding the kind of information that is needed. Check to see if there is any ambiguity, or if the respondents have any difficulty in responding. Administering the questionnaire personally and individually to a small group of respondents is usually the way to proceed with your pilot study.

The pilot instrument should invite comments about the perceived relevance of each question to the stated intent of the research. It would also be beneficial to provide a means for the respondent to suggest additional questions that the researcher did not include.

Cover Letter

If questionnaires are administered to an intact group such as students in a class or members of a congregation, then the investigator has the opportunity to inform the respondents of the intent of the study and motivate them to complete the questionnaire. However, when questionnaires are sent through the mail, it may be difficult to motivate respondents to fill out the questionnaire and to return it within a reasonable period of time. Unless the *potential* respondents believe that the questionnaire is of value, it is likely that they will become *non*-respondents. For this reason, a **cover letter** usually accompanies the questionnaire.

If the research is sponsored by a recognized group or a prestigious organization, this information should be stated in the cover letter since such information often adds credibility to the study.

The cover letter should also state that:

1. the questionnaire will not take a great deal of time to complete.

2. each individual's personal attention to the questionnaire is of extreme importance to the study.

In addition, the following ingredients would enhance the efficacy of a cover letter:

3. An introduction: The name of the researcher and the company, organization, or university that is requesting or approving this study.

4. A Purpose: The reason for conducting the study, the use for this questionnaire, and its value to the investigation should be explained. The sole intention of a study should not be to obtain a degree by means that include the use of this questionnaire [however important that is]. It is unlikely that a potential respondent will take the time to carefully fill out a questionnaire for this goal.

Note: You must also be careful not to reveal too much. This might bias the study and make the results invalid.

5. <u>A list of directions</u>: Explain how the questions are to be answered, how the questionnaire is to be returned, and if there is some reasonable deadline for returning it. Indicate whether or not the respondent needs to put his or her name on the form, and any other relevant information that should be included with the questionnaire.

6. <u>Return postage</u>: It is unreasonable to ask the respondent to answer your questionnaire and provide postage for its return to you.

The researcher should avoid the use of "obvious" form letters or letters where the initial salutation is:

Dear _____, *or "To Whom it may concern:"*

The letter should also be signed by the researcher personally.

Extra attention and a personal touch demonstrate the sincerity of the research effort and the importance of the respondents' participation.

Note: Without your taking the aforementioned information into consideration, it is likely that the questionnaire will only make it to the nearest trash receptacle.

cutting board:

    This would be an excellent time to create your cover letter. Insert a separate sheet of paper and compose your cover letter NOW! Check to see that you have incorporated the ideas suggested in this section.

Going the Extra Mile

Some ways to encourage respondents to perform the task of filling out the questionnaire, especially if the questionnaire is mailed, are:

1. Make personal contact by phone or in person, prior to sending out the questionnaire.

2. Offer some type of financial compensation or gift. (For short questionnaires, some companies put a questionnaire on the back of a small check).

3. Make the cover letter and questionnaire attractive looking.

4. Make the cover letter personal.

5. Make repeated contact with non-respondents.

A reasonable sequence of events may be:

1. About ten days after the initial mailing, mail all non-respondents a reminder card emphasizing the importance of the study and the need for a high response rate.

2. About ten days after the postcard is mailed, mail the remaining non-respondents a letter again emphasizing the importance of a high rate of return and including another questionnaire for those who threw the first one away.

3. If the response rate is still not satisfactory, it would be advisable to call non-respondents on the telephone or send a telegram or an e-mail.

The difficulties of getting the response rate to a reasonable level will depend on the nature of the sample, the nature of the study, the motivation of the people who are to complete the questionnaire, and the ease with which the questionnaire may be completed.

cutting board:

If you are planning to mail out questionnaires, which of the methods above do you think you will employ to increase the response rate? _____

The Personal Interview

The personal interview has many similarities to the questionnaire. The major advantages of using an interview instead of a questionnaire are:

1. The response rate is generally high.

2. It is an especially useful technique when dealing with children or an illiterate population.

3. It eliminates the misinterpretation of a question.

4. The subject is more likely to have clarified any misunderstandings.

5. It can encourage a relaxed conversation where questions can be asked in any order depending on the response of the interviewee.

6. It provides an opportunity to find out what people really think and believe about a certain topic through questioning.

7. It is more flexible and allows the interviewer to follow "leads" during the interview.

8. The interviewer can interpret body language as an extra source of information.

Note: A good interviewer has HEART: *H*onesty, *E*arnestness, *A*daptability, *R*eliability, and *T*rustworthiness.

Some disadvantages of the interview method are:

1. Time and economy: The expense and time involved in training interviewers and sending them to interview the respondents is greater than the expense and time of mailing questionnaires.

2. Reliability of information can be questioned because of interviewer bias.

3. Difficulties often arise in quantifying or statistically analyzing data obtained from interviews.

All surveys obtained through questionnaires or interviews adhere to the same ethical system: *The privacy of the individual is respected and weighed against the public's right to know.*

FOR YOUR INFORMATION AND EDUCATION:

The results of surveys that deal with sensitive issues are felt by many to be dubious. People are often not willing to reveal private details about their lives.

However, there is a statistical method that can allow investigators to ask questions in a way that is likely to elicit honest responses. This method was developed by Stanley Warner in 1965. It completely protects the privacy of individuals yet provides good survey information. It is called **randomized response**.

Suppose question (10) on a survey is: *"Have you used illegal drugs in the past week?"* The respondent is told to read the question

---

and flip a coin. He/she is to answer "NO" **only if** the coin comes up tails **and** they have not used illegal drugs. Otherwise, they should answer "YES." The proportion of the group that would have answered "NO" is then computed to be twice those that actually responded NO [The other half got heads], e.g., if 40% wrote NO then 80% (twice 40%) of the sample is determined to have not used illegal drugs in the past week, and 20% have used illegal drugs in the past week. People have commented that they trust this method in maintaining their privacy and are more willing to answer these questions honestly.

cutting board:

    1. If you are planning to use the personal interview, list the reasons for your decision:

_____

    2. Who will do the interviewing?

_____Why?_____

_____

Observation

Obtaining data through **observation**, both participant and non-participant, is becoming more and more common. It is perhaps the most direct means of finding out information, especially if your study is focused on deeds rather than words. The extent of your personal involvement depends on which of the two methods you choose.

In non-participant observation:

1. Your presence may be known or unknown.

2. You may observe through a device such as a one-way glass, or rely on observations from video or audio taping.

3. The data obtained tends to be fairly subjective.

The major advantage to using participant observation is that you can experience firsthand the psychological and social conditions that produce different decisions and practices.

The disadvantages to using participant observation are that

1. You could be influenced by your own interpretation and personal experiences.

2. Questions of reliability exists since others may interpret an experience differently than you.

3. Your presence might affect the subject and the situation being observed.

One way to reduce the disadvantages is to read your report to the people observed and to ask for comments, additions, or deletions prior to its formalization.

Accuracy is the key to making this type of data collection effective. Special training is needed to move from casual observer to systematic observer. In using structured observation techniques, the researcher usually searches for a relationship between independent variables to a dependent variable. The researcher must thus be able to code and recode data in a meaningful way, and be aware of the potential biases he/she brings to research.

FOR YOUR INFORMATION AND EDUCATION:

All methods of data collection have advantages and disadvantages compared to other methods. The method that you choose should be based upon the aims and objectives of the study and the population being studied. However, when you write your research paper you should include the advantages *and* disadvantages of the instrument you chose, and explain how you attempted to minimize the disadvantages.

Serving   Platters/Spices
[Statistics]
Featuring: What's Stat? (you say?)
How to Exhibit Your Date (a)
How to (Ap)praise Your Date (a)

What's Stat? (you say?)
Statistics is like trying to determine how many different colored m&m's are in a king size bag by looking at only a carefully selected handful.

The job of a statistician involves: **C O A I P**

1/2 cup	**C** OLLECTING
1/2 cup	**O** RGANIZING
1 cup	**A** NALYZING
1-2cups	**I** NTERPRETING
1 cup	**P** REDICTING

Statistics can be used to predict, but it is very important to understand that these predictions are not certainties. The fact that conclusions *may be incorrect* separates statistics from most other branches of mathematics. If a **fair** coin is tossed ten times and ten heads appear, the statistician would incorrectly report that the coin is biased. This conclusion, however, is not certain. It is only a "likely conclusion" reflecting the very low probability of getting ten heads in ten tosses.

After data are collected, they are used to produce various statistical numbers such as means, standard deviations, percentages, etc. These descriptive numbers summarize or describe the important characteristics of a known set of data. In hypothesis testing, descriptive numbers are standardized so that they can be compared to fixed values (found in tables or in computer programs) that indicate how "unusual" it is to obtain the data you collected. Once data are standardized and significance determined, you may be able to make inferences about an entire population (universe).

Note: Your Dissertation Cookbook intends to give you a substantial "taste" of statistics so that you will feel comfortable with this aspect of your "feast" preparation. You have already "nibbled" on statistics in the last section when you explored different methods of collecting data.

You might wish to seek further "condiments" to add to the knowledge you will acquire from your Dissertation Cookbook or consult with a statistician after reading the information in PHASE 2 to help you decide which statistics, if any, would be applicable to your study. We urge you to use statistical programs or business calculators to perform the tedious computations that often arise during statistical testing. Remember: You are ultimately responsible for the results. You must be aware of why you are using a certain test, know what assumptions are made when such a test is used, understand what the test results indicate, and understand how this analysis fits in with your study.

The Role Of Statistics

Statistics is merely a tool. It is not the be-all and end-all for the researcher. Those who insist that research is not research unless it is statistical display a myopic view of the research process. These are often the same folks who are equally adamant that unless research is "experimental research" it is not research.

One cardinal rule applies: *The nature of the data governs the method that is appropriate to interpret the data and the tool of research that is required to process those data.* A historian seeking to answer problems associated with the assassination of Dr. Martin Luther King, Jr., would be hard put to produce either a statistical or an experimental study, and yet the research of the historian can be quite as scholarly and scientifically respectable as that of any quantitative or experimental study.

Statistics many times describes a quasi-world rather than the real world. You might find that the mean grade for a class is 82 but not one student actually received a grade of 82. Consider the person that found out that the average family has 1.75 children and with heartfelt gratitude exclaimed: "Boy, am I grateful that I was the first born!" What is accepted statistically is sometimes meaningless empirically. *However, statistics is a useful mechanism and a means of panning precious simplicity from the sea of complexity.* It is a tool that can be applied to practically every discipline!

Frequently Asked Questions About Statistics:

1. What is the purpose of statistics?

The purpose of statistics is to collect, organize, and analyze data (from a sample), interpret the results and try to make predictions (about a population). We "do" statistics when we COAIP-- collect, organize, analyze, interpret, and predict -- data. One relies on statistics to determine "how close" to what one anticipated would happen actually did happen.

2. Why and how would one use inferential statistics?

In inferential statistics we compare a numerical result to a number that is reflective of a chance happening, and determine how significant the difference between these two numbers is.

3. Are predictions indisputable in statistics?

Statistics can be used to predict, but these predictions are not certainties. Statistics offers us a "best guess." The fact that conclusions may be *incorrect* separates statistics from most other branches of mathematics. If a *fair* coin is tossed ten times and ten heads appear, the statistician would incorrectly report that the coin is biased. This conclusion, however, is not certain. It is only a "likely conclusion," reflecting the very low probability of getting ten heads in ten tosses.

4. What are hypotheses?

Hypotheses are educated guesses that are derived by logical analysis using induction or deduction from one's knowledge of the problem and from the purpose for conducting a study. They can range from very general statements to highly specific ones. Most research studies focus on the proving or the disproving of hypotheses.

5. What is statistical hypothesis testing?

Statistical hypothesis testing or tests of significance are used to determine if the differences between two or more descriptive statistics (such as a mean, percent, proportion, standard deviation, etc.) are statistically significant or more likely due to chance variations. It is a method of testing claims made about populations by using a sample from that population. In hypothesis testing, descriptive numbers are standardized so that they can be compared to fixed values (found in tables or in computer programs) that indicate how "unusual" it is to obtain the data collected. A statistical hypothesis to be tested is always written as a null hypothesis (no change). An appropriate test will tell us to either reject the null hypothesis or fail to reject (accept) the null hypothesis.

6. Once I find a test that helps to test my hypothesis, is there anything else I need to be concerned about?

Certain conditions are necessary prior to initiating a statistical test. One important condition is the distribution of the data. Once data are standardized and the significance level determined, a statistical test can be performed to analyze the data and possibly make inferences about an entire population (universe).

7. What are "p" values?

A p-value (or probability value) is the probability of getting a value of the sample test statistics that is at least as extreme as the one found from the sample data, assuming the null hypothesis is true. Traditionally, statisticians used "alpha" values that set up a dichotomy: reject/fail to reject conclusion. P-values measure how confident we are in rejecting a null hypothesis. If a p-value is less than 0.01 we say this is "highly statistically significant" and there is very strong evidence *against* the null hypothesis. P- values between 0.01 and 0.05 indicate that a result is statistically significant and adequate evidence against the null hypothesis. For p-values greater than 0.05, there is insufficient evidence against the null hypothesis.

8. What is the difference between a parametric and a nonparametric test?

Most of the more well known statistical tests use parametric methods. These methods generally require strict restrictions such as:
    1. The data should be rational or interval. [Data comes in four types and four levels of measurement which can be remembered by the French word for black: NOIR - nominal (lowest) ordinal, interval, and rational (highest)].

Measurement Scales		Characteristics
	NOIR	
Non-Interval Scales	Nominal Scale	Measures in terms of name of designations or discrete units or categories
	Ordinal Scale	Measures in terms of such values as more or less, larger or smaller, but without specifying the size of the intervals
Interval Scales	Interval Scale	Measures in terms of equal intervals or degrees of difference but without a zero point. Ratios do not apply
	Ratio Scale	Measures in terms of equal intervals and an absolute zero point of origin. Ratios apply

A general and important guideline is that statistics based on one level of measurement should not be used for a lower level, but can be used for a higher level. An implication of this guideline is that data obtained from using a Likert-type scale should not be used in most parametric tests. The good news is that there is almost always an alternative approach using nonparametric methods.

2. The sample data must come from a normally distributed population.

Note: One of the most important characteristics of the shape of a distribution is whether the distribution is skewed or symmetrical. Skewness is important in that increasing Skewness causes the mean to be less acceptable and useful as the measure of central tendency. Many parametric statistical tests requires a normal distribution of the data. Graphical methods such as histograms are very helpful in identifying Skewness in a distribution.

   If the mean, median, and mode are identical, then the shape of the distribution will be unimodal and symmetric, and will resemble a normal distribution. A distribution that is skewed to the right and unimodal will have a long right tail, whereas a distribution that is skewed to the left and unimodal will have a long left tail. A unimodal distribution that is skewed has its mean, median, and mode occur at different values. For highly skewed distributions, the median is the preferred measure of central tendency, since a mean can be greatly affected by a few extreme values on one end.

Kurtosis is a parameter that describes whether the particular distribution concentrates its probability in a central peak or in the tails. Normal populations lie at 3 on this scale, non-normal populations lie on either side of 3.

Good things about nonparametric methods:

1. Can be applied to a wider variety of situations and are distribution free.

2. Can be used with nominal and ranked data.

3. Use simpler computations and can be easier to understand.

Not so good things about nonparametric methods:

1. Tend to waste information since most of the information is reduced to qualitative form.

2. Generally less sensitive so may need stronger evidence to show significance, that could me larger samples are needed.

How to Exhibit Your Date (a)

Data which are collected but not organized are often referred to as "raw" data. It is common to seek a means by which the human mind can easily assimilate and summarize "raw" data. Frequency tables and graphs delectably fulfill this purpose.

FOR YOUR INFORMATION AND EDUCATION:

A **frequency table** is so named because it lists categories of scores along with their corresponding frequencies. This is an extremely simple and effective means of organizing data for further evaluation. For a large collection of scores, it might be best to use a statistical program such as <u>Statview, SPSS, GBSTAT</u>, etc., where you enter the raw data into your computer and then with the mere press of a button or two, construct an awesome frequency table.

If the data you obtained are **demographic** (about personal characteristics or geographical regions), then it would be beneficial to present the percentages of these characteristics within the sample (e.g., 24% of the subjects studied were Latino). If you determine an arithmetic mean in your study, then both the mean and the standard deviation should be presented.

FOR YOUR INFORMATION AND EDUCATION:

The **standard deviation** or the square root of the **variance**, is considered to be the most important measure of dispersion about a mean. Data are normally distributed about the mean, that is, most of your data will be within (1) standard deviation of the mean. If the mean score for a group of students who took the S.A.T is 500, and the standard deviation is 50, most of the S.A.T. scores of the people in this group will be 500 + or - 50, i.e., between 450 and 550.

Data are often represented in pictorial form by means of a graph. Some common types of graphs include, **pie charts** (if you are picturing the relationship of parts to a whole), **histograms** (if you are displaying the different types of numerical responses with respect to the frequency in which they occur. A histogram is similar to a **bar graph** which is often used to represent the frequency of nominal data), **ogives** (if you are displaying cumulative frequencies such as incomes under $10,000), or **stem and leaf plots** (If you wish that the actual data be preserved and used to form a picture of the distribution).

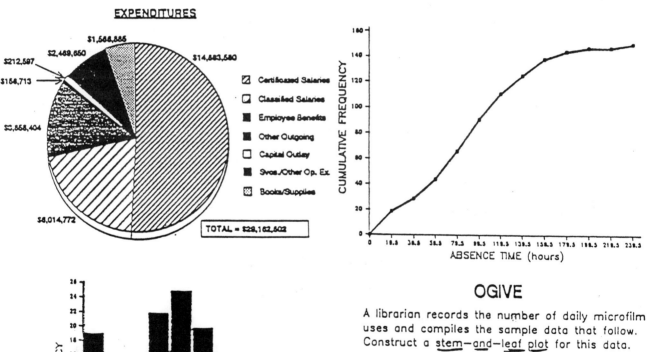

OGIVE

A librarian records the number of daily microfilm uses and compiles the sample data that follow. Construct a stem—and—leaf plot for this data.

10 11 15 23 27 28 38 38 39 39
40 41 44 45 46 46 52 57 58 65

STEM	LEAF
1	015
2	378
3	8899
4	014566
5	278
6	5

cutting board:

1. Arrange your data in a frequency table. (If you have administered a questionnaire, you might wish to list the different responses to each question in conjunction with the frequency that they were selected.)

2. Construct appropriate graphs to picture the distributions determined by your frequency table.

3. Compute any statistical numbers that are **descriptive** of your data such as means, standard deviations, proportions, percents, quartiles, etc. [You may wish to use a calculator or a computer that is programmed to determine your mean and standard deviation with the mere press of a button once information has been entered in a befitting manner. The manual that comes with the machine or computer program could prove helpful for this task.]

Note: Statistical computer programs can instantaneously produce frequency tables; compute means, percentages, standard deviations; and generate suitable graphs reflecting your findings once you have appropriately input raw data. [They never complain about doing any of these things.] By a click of a mouse you can order a statistical test and in under a second know whether to accept or fail to accept your statistical hypothesis!

Assistant Chefs
Identifying Your **Population** and
Choosing Your **Sample**

Most chefs employ a variety of people to assist them in producing an elegant banquet. Similarly, most researchers depend upon other people to help them obtain the information they need to prepare their dissertation or research report.

If you are planning to conduct a survey or interview people, you need to get "enough" people whose views count. Usually it is not practical or possible to study the entire **universe, or population**, so you might need to settle for a

sample, or a subset of the universe. In choosing a sample and a method of data collection, you need to ask yourself certain questions:

1. How quickly are the data needed?

2. What are the resources available?

3. Should probability or non-probability sampling be used?

The three most common methods of sampling are:

1. Simple random sampling.

Simple random sampling is accomplished when each member of the universe has the exact same chance of being selected. This can be accomplished by first establishing a proper sampling frame or a list of all the members in the universal population being studied. For example, if you plan to sample the pupils at a particular high school, then a collection of the names of all students in the high school would be needed.

The next phase could be to assign a number to all the members of the population. A random number generator either electronic, through dice, or using some set of digits from a telephone directory could be used to generate the sample. Whenever duplicate numbers come up, they are discarded. Another method of generating a random sample is to put all names in a box, shake the box, and pull out a name. This name should be recorded and then tossed back in the box. Should the same name be selected more than one time before the sample is obtained, it should be disregarded. [This is called "sampling with replacement" and guarantees that the requirement "each member has the same chance of being selected," is met.]

Sometimes it is not possible to gain access to the entire population so that you may need to settle for a smaller sub population. If this is the case, the researcher should try to randomize as much as possible within that sub population.

2. Systematic stratified sampling

In **systematic stratified sampling,** you draw a sample with a pattern of important characteristics. Members of the population are subdivided into at least two different sub populations or strata e.g. gender. Samples are then drawn from each stratum. If you are surveying a high school whose student population is 40% of Mexican decent, you might wish your sample to reflect that same population by dividing the population into ethnic groups and obtaining a set percentage from each group.
In **cluster sampling**, members of the population are divided into sections (or clusters), randomly select a few of those sections, are randomly

selected and then all the members for the selected sections are chosen. For example, in conducting a preelection poll we could randomly select 30 election precincts and survey *all* people from those precincts. The results may need to be adjusted to correct for any disproportionate representation of groups. Used extensively by government and private research organizations.

3. Non-probability sampling

Non-probability sampling is something we all use in every day life. If you want to try out a new brand of crackers, you know that you only need to choose one cracker from one box to decide if you like the cracker because the others can beexpected to taste pretty much the same. Another common form of non-probability sampling may be carried out when trying to conduct "on the street" interviews. Researchers will often have some bias towards which people they will sample.

In **convenience sampling** one uses subjects that are readily available. Sometimes this is quite good - -e.g., a teacher wanting to know about left-handed students needs would not include those who are right-handed. However, such sampling can be seriously biased when researchera choose only those they feel comfortable working with.

Sometimes non-probability sampling is done inadvertently. Back in 1933 a telephone poll indicated that Landon would overwhelmingly become our next president. He disn't. What became obvious, after this study was analyzed, was that it failed to take into account that Republicans had most of the phones in 1933 and that Roosevelt's supporters were the majority without telephones.

If a non-probability survey is to be conducted, you must be very careful not to generalize too much from it. It is, however, very useful in the early stages of developing your study in order to get some new ideas and in the development of some interview questions, in practicing interviews and surveying techniques, or in a pilot study. At times, only a small sample of the population is available to participate in a study.

Non-probability samples are usually easier to obtain, but the gains in efficiency are often matched with losses in accuracy and generality.

Sometimes thousands of people are sampled to get the data needed; on other occasions, a sample may be as small as one.

Some factors effecting the size of a sample are:

1. the size of the universe or population being studied;

2. the purpose of the study;

3. the potential application of the result of the study;

4. the type of statistical tests; and

5. the research techniques being used.

With a relatively large sample you are usually able to see the general, overall pattern but since in many tests the significance of measures is a function of sample size, it is possible to get a statistically significant relation when the strength of the relationship is too small to be used. Under sound statistical practices using simple random samples obtained through probability means, you can often get excellent information from a sample size of 30 or less.

Sometimes a **case study** of one or two subjects is the most appropriate means of conducting an investigation. This enables you to obtain detailed information about a problem in which there is much interest but little information.

Case studies are usually selected by non-probability sampling according to your judgment about whether the sample is a good representative of the population. For example, most information obtained about the (Idiot) Savant-Syndrome has been obtained through individual case studies of these extraordinary people.

FOR YOUR INFORMATION AND EDUCATION:

Another very important part of sampling is the **non-response rate.** This sector includes those people who could not be contacted or who refused to answer questions. A general rule is to try to keep the non-response rate under 25%. To keep the non-response rate small, you could ask the assistance of a community leader, and have that person explain the purpose and importance of your study in great detail to the potential respondents.

The size of the survey may be decided with statistical precision. A major concern in choosing a sample size is that it should be large "enough" so that it will be representative of the population from which it comes and from which you wish to make inferences. It ought to be large enough so that important differences can be found in subgroups such as men and women, democrats and republicans, groups receiving treatment and control groups, etc.

Two major issues to be considered when using statistical methods to choose sample size are concern with sampling error and confidence levels.

Sampling error. Some small differences will almost always exist among samples and between them and the population from which they are drawn. One approach to measuring sample error is to report the *standard error of measurement* which is computed by dividing the population standard deviation (if known) by the square root of the sample size. Minimizing sampling error helps to maximize the sample's representativeness.

Example: If the Stanford-Binet I.Q. test (where standard deviation is 15) is administered to 100 subjects then the standard error of the mean would be: 15/10 or 1.5

Confidence Levels. You will need to decide how "confident" you wish, or need, to be that your sample is representative of the population. Frequently, the 95% confidence level is chosen. This means that there is a 95% chance that the sample and the population will look alike and a 5% chance that they will not.

Note: We can use the following formula to determine the sample size necessary to discover the "true" mean value from a population:

$$n = [(z)(\sigma) / e]^2$$

where z corresponds to a confidence level (found on a table or computer program). Some common **z** values are 1.645 or 1.96, which might reflect a 95% confidence level (depending on the statistical hypothesis under investigation), and 2.33, which could reflect a 99% confidence level in a one tailed-test and 2.575 for a two-tailed test. σ is the standard deviation, and e is the margin of error.

Example: If we need to be 99% confident that we are within 0.25 lbs of a true mean weight of babies in an infant care facility, and σ = 1.1, we would need to sample 129 babies:

$$n = [2.575 \ (1.1)/ \ 0.25]^2 = 128.3689 \text{ or } 129.$$

Note: A formula that we can use to determine the sample size necessary to test a hypothesis involving percentages is:

$$n = (z/e)^2 \ (p) \ (1-p)$$

where n = sample size, **z** = standard score corresponding to a certain confidence level. We represent the proportion of sampling error by "e," and the estimated proportion or incidence of cases by "p."

Example: It is estimated that 87% of North American adults have some level of mathematics anxiety. To compare and contrast math anxious and non-math anxious adults with a 95% confidence level (**z** = 1.96) we will need to test 44 North American adults:

$$n = (1.96/.10)^2 \ (.87) \ (0.13) = 384.16 \ (0.1131) = 44$$

cutting board:

    1. What is the population and sample that you will be studying?
_____

    2. How will you select your sample? Why?
_____

    3. What measures will you take to see that your sample size is adequate for your study? _____
_____

How to (ap)praise your Date (a)
STATISTICAL HYPOTHESIS TESTING
1 c Analyzing
1 c Interpreting
1 c Predicting

- sss **CANDOALL -- An EZ model for Statistical Hypothesis Testing**
- **How to Choose Desirable Spices (tests)**
- **Testing Claims About:**
    **means, standard deviations,
    proportions, and relations.**

In this section we will be exploring **Statistical Hypothesis Testing** *to determine "how close" to what you anticipated would happen actually did happen.*

Hypotheses are educated guesses that are derived by logical analysis using induction or deduction from your knowledge of the problem and from your purpose for conducting the study. They can range from very general statements to highly specific ones. Most research studies focus on the proving or the disproving of hypotheses.

After the data have been collected and organized in some logical manner such as a frequency table and a **descriptive statistic** (mean, standard deviation, percentage, etc.) is computed, then a statistical test is often utilized to analyze the data, interpret what this analysis means in terms of the problem, and make predictions based on these interpretations.

You might wish to visit this section once before all your data is collected and then plan a revisit once your data is known.

Note: When you use statistics you are comparing <u>your numerical results</u> to a number that is reflective of a <u>chance happening</u> and determining how significant the <u>difference</u> between these two numbers is.

If you are planning to use statistical hypotheses testing as part of your dissertation (research project), you should read this section slowly and carefully, paying close attention to key words and phrases. Make sure you are familiar with all the terminology employed.

Note: If your study involves quantitative data and the testing of hypotheses, you will undoubtedly find the examples in this part of the Dissertation Cookbook extremely beneficial. It is our intent to familiarize you with the techniques of the statistician and help you determine which statistical tests would work best for *your* study. Remember to keep a positive mental attitude as well as an open and inquisitive mind as you digest the information in this section.

There is a myth that statistical analysis is a difficult process which requires an advanced degree. This need not be the case. Statistical hypothesis testing can be fun and easy.

Although many esoteric tests exist (just as there are many exotic spices in the universe), most researchers use mundane tests (the way most chefs prepare delicious meals with common spices). The mundane "spices" for statistical hypothesis testing are: z-tests, t-tests, chi-square tests, F-tests, and rho-tests.

As you carefully and cheerfully read through this section you will learn which of these "spices" might best complement your meal. Just as in cooking, sometimes you will find more than one spice that could be apropos and could enhance your meal. In analyzing your data you will likely find more than one type of statistical test that would be appropriate for your study, and the choice is often yours to make.

TESTING A CLAIM ABOUT A MEAN

The example in this section will be testing a claim about a mean obtained from a sample. If you can answer yes to one or more of the questions below, you could use this *identical* statistical test in your study

Are you claiming that:

___1. A new product, program, or treatment is better than an existing one?

___2. An existing product, program, or treatment is not what it professes to be?

___3. A group is under (or over) achieving?

Note: The recipe in this section can be used to check **any** statistical hypothesis (not just a statistical hypothesis about a mean), so it would behoove you to read through the following example **with eager anticipation and note any similarities between this study and your study**.

Example: Ms. Rodriguez (Ms. R) has found a new method of teaching reading (NMTR) that she claims is better than traditional methods. The average seventh grader reads at a 7.5 reading level by mid-year. Ms. R claims that NMTR will increase the average reading level significantly by mid- year.

To test her claim, Ms. R samples 36 students (N= 36) who have been using NMTR and finds that by mid year the mean average of this group is 7.8. However, since the standard deviation of the population is 0.76 this could indicate that the sample students are just within normal boundaries.

Statistical hypothesis testing will be used to determine if the sample mean score of 7.8 represents a statistically *significant* increase from the population mean of 7.5, or if the difference is more likely due to chance variations in reading scores.

Before the (8) step statistical test "recipe" is employed, you need to procure three preliminary pieces of information - each beginning with the letter s.

(s_1) What is the substantive hypothesis?
       [What does the researcher think will happen?]

Ms. R claims that NMTR will significantly increase the average reading level of seventh grade students by mid year.

cutting board:

Write one substantive hypothesis that is apropos to your study, i.e., what do you think (claim) that your study will reveal?

_____
_____
_____

s_2) How large is the sample that was studied?

Ms. R sampled 36 seventh grade students (n= 36) who have been using NMTR

s_3) What descriptive statistic was determined by the sample?

The mean average of the sample, $\bar{x}$, was 7.8.

cutting board:

1.   Determine the sample size for your study. n = _____.

2.   What descriptive statistic was obtained from your study? _____ (You may wish to give an approximate value or result that you *think* you *might* obtain from your study to practice applying this process.)_____

Now we are ready to take the information obtained by the three s's and employ an (8) step recipe to create a "delicious" statistical test, using the CANDOALL model.

We will determine if Ms. R's claim, "NMTR increases the reading level of seventh graders," is statistically correct.

1. (C) Identify the <u>C</u>laim to be tested and express it in symbolic form. The claim is about the population and that is reflected by the Greek letter μ.

$$\mu > 7.5$$

That is, Ms. R claims that the mean reading score, μ, of the seventh grade students who have used NMTR is greater than the population mean, 7.5

cutting board:

Write your claim in symbolic form.

---

2. (A) Express in symbolic form the statement that would be true, the <u>A</u>lternative to the claim, if the original claim is false. All cases must be covered.

$$\mu \leq 7.5$$

cutting board:

Write the opposite of your claim in symbolic form. (remember to cover all possibilities).

---

3. (N) Identify the <u>N</u>ull and alternative statistical hypothesis.

Note: The null statistical hypothesis should be the one that contains *no* change (an equal sign).

H_0: $\mu \leq 7.5$ (Null statistical hypothesis)
H_1: $\mu > 7.5$ (Alternative statistical hypothesis)

cutting board:

    Determine the null and alternative hypotheses in your
study. _____
_____

Note: A statistical test is designed to <u>accept</u> or <u>reject</u> (*aka* fail to accept) the statistical **null hypothesis** being examined.

4. (D) <u>D</u>ecide on the level of significance, alpha (α), based on the seriousness of a "type I error" which is the mistake of rejecting the null hypothesis when it is in fact true. Make alpha small if the consequences of rejecting a true alpha are severe. The smaller the alpha value, the less likely you will be to reject the null hypothesis. Alpha values 0.05 and 0.01 are very common.

$$\alpha = 0.05$$

FOR YOUR INFORMATION AND EDUCATION:

    Some researchers do not use **alpha** values (which are pre-determined at the beginning of a statistical test and indicate <u>acceptable</u> levels of significance). Instead, they obtain **p** values (which indicate <u>actual levels</u> of significance of a claim and leave the conclusion as to whether this is "significant enough" to the reader). It is possible to do both (set α and compute **p**) and then compare these two values when reporting your findings.

Note: It would be a good idea to find out if "α" or "**p**" values are preferred within your profession. You could easily determine this by consulting journals in your discipline or by calling your professional organization's research department.

cutting board:

Set **alpha** levels (α) for your study or indicate that you will be using only **p** values._____

5. (O) O̲rder a statistical test relevant to your study (see Table 1).

Since the claim involves a sample mean and n > 30, table (1) assures us that we can compute a Z value and use a Z test. That sounds great, you say, but what does it mean? A **Z** value is a number we compute which can then be graphed as a point on the horrizontal scale of the standard normal distribution curve. This point indicates how far from the population mean our sample mean is, and thus enables us to determine how "unusual" our research findings are.

FOR YOUR INFORMATION AND EDUCATION:

The **Central Limit Theorem** implies that for samples of sizes larger than 30, the sample means can be approximated reasonably well by a normal (z) distribution. The approximation gets better as the sample size, N, becomes larger.

When you compute a **Z** value you are converting your mean to a mean of **0** and your standard deviation to a standard deviation of **1**. This allows you to use the standard normal distribution curve and its corresponding table to determine the significance of your values, regardless of the actual value of your mean or standard deviation.

A **standard normal probability distribution** is a bell-shaped curve (also called a **Gaussian curve** in honor of its discoverer, Karl Gauss) where the mean or middle value is 0, and the standard deviation, the place where the curve starts to bend, is equal to 1 on the right and -1 on the left. The area under every probability distribution curve is equal to 1 or 100%). Since a Gaussian curve is symmetric about the mean, it is important to note that the mean divides this curve into two equal areas of 50%.

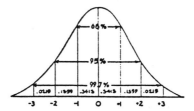

Blood cholesterol levels, heights of adult women, weights of 10 year old boys, diameters of apples, scores on standardized test, etc., are all examples of collections of values whose **frequency distributions** resemble the Gaussian curve.

If you were to record all the possible outcomes from the toss of 100 different coins by graphing the number of heads that could occur on the horizontal axis (0,1,2,3...100), and the frequency with which each of the number of heads could occur on the vertical axis, you will produce a graph resembling the normal distribution. (The most "frequent" results would cluster around 50 heads and become less and less frequent as you consider values further and further from 50.]

6. (A) Perform the **A**rithmetic: determine the test statistic, the critical value (s), and the critical region

The sample mean of **7.8** is equivalent to a z value of **2.37**. This **z** value is the test statistic, and was computed using the following formula:

$$z = \frac{\bar{X} - \mu}{\sigma / \sqrt{n}}$$

X = sample mean, μ = population mean, n = size of sample
σ = population standard deviation,
Thus, **z = (7.8 - 7.5) / (0.76)/6 = 2.37** (to the nearest hundredth)

If you would like to verify this computation on your calculator, you could first compute

The Dissertation Cookbook   101

$$\sigma / \sqrt{n}$$

that is, the standard deviation, 0.76, divided by 6 (which is the square root of of our n of 36), and put or store the quotient in *Memory +*. Next, enter 0.3 (which is the difference between the sample mean and the population mean), and divide this entry by *Memory Recall*.

Note: z numbers usually vary between -3 and +3. If they are outside of this range the null hypothesis will almost always be rejected (or an error was made).
Note: $\sigma / \sqrt{n}$ (sigma divided by the square root of n) is often called the **standard error of the mean** or the standard deviation of the sample means.
Note: Most times you can substitute the actual standard deviation of the sample, **s**, for the population standard deviation, σ, if σ is unknown.

The $\underline{\alpha = 0.05}$ level employs us to find a **z** value that will separate the curve into 2 unequal regions; the smaller one with an area of **0.05** (5%), and the larger one with an area of 100% - 5% or 95% (0.95). (Often referred to as a 95% confidence level).

Z values indicate the per cent of area under the bell-shaped curve from the mean (middle) towards the "right tail" of the curve. Thus, for an alpha of 0.05, we need to determine what **z** value will cut off an area of 45% (0.4500) from the mean towards the "right tail" (we already know that 50% of the area is on the left side of the mean. We obtain 95% by adding 45% to 50%).

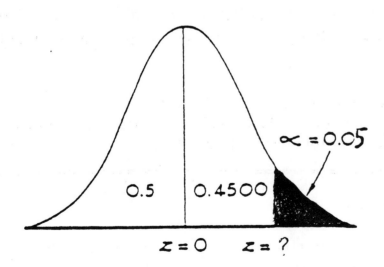

"Hunting" through the vast array of four digit numerals in the table, we find our critical value to be between 1.6 (see **z** column) + 0.04 (1.64) which (reading down the .04 column) determines an area of **0.4495**, and 1.6 +.05 (1.65) which determines an area of **0.4505**. Thus, if we take the mean average of 1.64 and 1.65, we can blissfully determine the critical value to be <u>1.645</u>. and the critical region to be all **Z** values <u>greater than 1.645</u>. This determination requires us to reject the null hypothesis if our test statistics (**Z** value) is greater than 1.645.

Note Since there is only **one** alternative hypothesis, $H_1 : \mu > 7.5$, we call this is a **one-tailed (right tailed) test** If our alternative hypothesis was $\mu \neq 7.5$ a **two-tailed test** would be used since there would be **two** alternatives: $\mu < 7.5$ or $\mu > 7.5$.

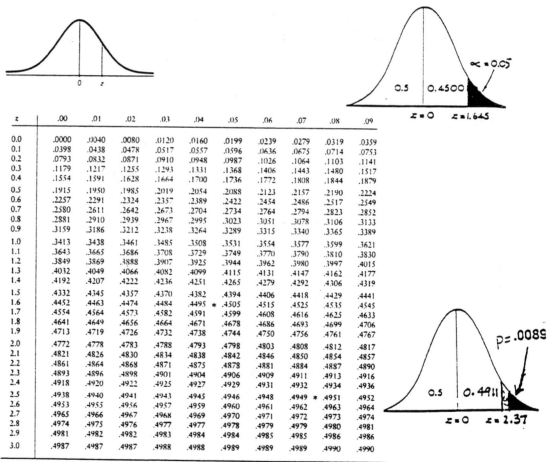

z	.00	.01	.02	.03	.04	.05	.06	.07	.08	.09
0.0	.0000	.0040	.0080	.0120	.0160	.0199	.0239	.0279	.0319	.0359
0.1	.0398	.0438	.0478	.0517	.0557	.0596	.0636	.0675	.0714	.0753
0.2	.0793	.0832	.0871	.0910	.0948	.0987	.1026	.1064	.1103	.1141
0.3	.1179	.1217	.1255	.1293	.1331	.1368	.1406	.1443	.1480	.1517
0.4	.1554	.1591	.1628	.1664	.1700	.1736	.1772	.1808	.1844	.1879
0.5	.1915	.1950	.1985	.2019	.2054	.2088	.2123	.2157	.2190	.2224
0.6	.2257	.2291	.2324	.2357	.2389	.2422	.2454	.2486	.2517	.2549
0.7	.2580	.2611	.2642	.2673	.2704	.2734	.2764	.2794	.2823	.2852
0.8	.2881	.2910	.2939	.2967	.2995	.3023	.3051	.3078	.3106	.3133
0.9	.3159	.3186	.3212	.3238	.3264	.3289	.3315	.3340	.3365	.3389
1.0	.3413	.3438	.3461	.3485	.3508	.3531	.3554	.3577	.3599	.3621
1.1	.3643	.3665	.3686	.3708	.3729	.3749	.3770	.3790	.3810	.3830
1.2	.3849	.3869	.3888	.3907	.3925	.3944	.3962	.3980	.3997	.4015
1.3	.4032	.4049	.4066	.4082	.4099	.4115	.4131	.4147	.4162	.4177
1.4	.4192	.4207	.4222	.4236	.4251	.4265	.4279	.4292	.4306	.4319
1.5	.4332	.4345	.4357	.4370	.4382	.4394	.4406	.4418	.4429	.4441
1.6	.4452	.4463	.4474	.4484	.4495 *	.4505	.4515	.4525	.4535	.4545
1.7	.4554	.4564	.4573	.4582	.4591	.4599	.4608	.4616	.4625	.4633
1.8	.4641	.4649	.4656	.4664	.4671	.4678	.4686	.4693	.4699	.4706
1.9	.4713	.4719	.4726	.4732	.4738	.4744	.4750	.4756	.4761	.4767
2.0	.4772	.4778	.4783	.4788	.4793	.4798	.4803	.4808	.4812	.4817
2.1	.4821	.4826	.4830	.4834	.4838	.4842	.4846	.4850	.4854	.4857
2.2	.4861	.4864	.4868	.4871	.4875	.4878	.4881	.4884	.4887	.4890
2.3	.4893	.4896	.4898	.4901	.4904	.4906	.4909	.4911	.4913	.4916
2.4	.4918	.4920	.4922	.4925	.4927	.4929	.4931	.4932	.4934	.4936
2.5	.4938	.4940	.4941	.4943	.4945	.4946	.4948	.4949 *	.4951	.4952
2.6	.4953	.4955	.4956	.4957	.4959	.4960	.4961	.4962	.4963	.4964
2.7	.4965	.4966	.4967	.4968	.4969	.4970	.4971	.4972	.4973	.4974
2.8	.4974	.4975	.4976	.4977	.4977	.4978	.4979	.4979	.4980	.4981
2.9	.4981	.4982	.4982	.4983	.4984	.4984	.4985	.4985	.4986	.4986
3.0	.4987	.4987	.4987	.4988	.4988	.4989	.4989	.4989	.4990	.4990

Note: The p value is .0089. We arrived at this value quite easily. Recall, in step 6 we computed the *relation between variables* score to be **2.37**. If you go down the left side of the table and find a z value of 2.3, then going across to the .07 column, you find the number **0.4911**. This indicates an area of **49.11%** from the mean **z** value of 0 to the **z** value of 2.37. Thus, 50% + 49.11% or **99.11%** of the area of the curve is to the left of 2.37 and the small tail to the right of 2.37 has an area of 100% - 99.11% = **0.89%** or **0.0089,** which is our p-value.

7. (L) Look to reject the null hypothesis (aka fail to accept) if the test statistic is in the critical region. Fail to reject the null hypothesis (aka to accept) if the test statistic is not in the critical region.

Ms. R's **z** value is in the critical region since 2.37 > 1.645. Thus we will reject the null hypothesis.

cutting board:

---

8. (L) In Lay (simple and nontechnical) terms, restate the previous conclusion.

We have reason to believe that NMTR improves the reading level of seventh grade students.

FOR YOUR INFORMATION AND EDUCATION:

If your sample size is less than 30 and the population standard deviation is unknown, but there is a normal distribution in the population, then you can compute a "t" statistic, where:

$$t = \frac{\bar{x} - \mu}{s/\sqrt{n}}$$

and s is the standard deviation of the sample, μ is the mean under contention, and n is the size of the sample.

Notice that **Z** and **T** statistics are computed exactly the same way, the only difference is in their corresponding values of significance when you (or your computer) check these values on the graph or table.

In this example we tested a claim about a numerical value; mean test scores on a standardized test. The sample data came from a population which was known to have a normal distribution. We were thus able to use **parametric methods** in our hypothesis testing.

In general, when you test claims about interval or rational parameters (such as mean, standard deviation, or proportions), and some fairly strict requirements (such as the sample data has come from a normally distributed population) are met, you should be able to use parametric methods.

If you do not meet the necessary requirements for parametric methods, do not despair. It is very likely that there are alternative techniques, named appropriately, **nonparametric methods** which you will be able to use instead.

Since they do not require normally distributed populations, nonparametric tests are often called **distribution-free tests**. Some advantages to using nonparametric methods include:

1. They can often be applied to nominal data that lack exact numerical values.

2. They usually involve computations that are simpler than the corresponding parametric methods.

3. They tend to be easier to understand.

Unfortunately, there are the following disadvantages:

1. Nonparametric methods tend to "waste" information, since exact numerical data are often reduced to a qualitative form. Some treat all values as either positive (+) or negative (-). [A dieter using this test would count a loss of 50 lbs as the same as a loss of 2 lbs.]

2. They are generally less sensitive than the corresponding parametric methods. This means that you need stronger evidence before rejecting the null hypothesis, or larger sample sizes.

cutting board:

1. My data are best described as:

   A. Parametric (deals only with numbers that are integers or rationals).

   B. Non- Parametric (deals with ordered numbers, rankings, or names only).

2. Checking with Table (1), I find that the most appropriate Statistical Test(s) to check the validity of my hypothesis will be:

_____

*TABLE 1
*TABLE 1
Recommended methods of cooking
STATISTICAL HYPOTHESIS TESTING

MY CLAIM IS ABOUT A:	SAMPLE CLAIM	ASSUMPTION	PARAMETRIC TEST-/STATISTIC	NONPARAMETRIC TEST/STATISTIC
mean	Class A has a higher IQ than average.	$n \geq 30$ or s.d known / $n < 30$, s.d. unknown	z / t	Sign Test / Wilcox/Mann Whitney U (U)
proportion	75% of voters prefer candidate	$np > 5$ and $nq > 5$	z	
standard deviation	This instrument has less errors than others	normal population	x^2	Kruskal-Wallis (H)
two means	EZ diet is more effective than DF diet?	dependent / independent	t / t or z	Sign Test / U

(A low t or U value would indicate proportions are similar.)

two standard deviations	The ages of group A are more homogeneous than the ages of group B.		f	H
two proportions	There are more Democrats in Chicago than in LA.		z	Sign Test
relationship between 2 variables	Smoking related to cancer. (If r is close to 0, then no relation)		Pearson r	Spearman r
Are two variables dependent?			f	H
How close do ex- pwctws values agree with observed (aka goodness of fit)	k variables		x^2 df = k-1	
ANOVA comparing 3 or more means	(compute: variances between sample means/total variances) df: num:=(k - 1) den = k(n-1);K= no. of groups n= amt in each group		f	H

Contingency table: A table of observed frequencies where the rows correspond to one variable and the columns another. It is used to see if two variables are dependent but cannot be used to determine what the relationship is between the two variables.

STUDY OF 1000 DEATHS OF MALES

	Cancer	Heart Disease	Other
Smoking	135	310	205
Non-Smoking	55	155	140

Note: x^2 would be computed. A large x^2 value indicates there is a relation between variables

cutting board:

If you are using a **z** or **t**-test, use the curve below to put in your test statistics, critical points, and critical regions.

cutting board: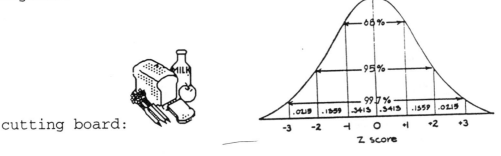

The non-parametric counterpart of both the t and z tests is: the **Sign Test**

We are now going to examine some felicitous applications for other statistical tests. You might wish to scan the list and see if you can identify similarities between the examples given and any of the hypotheses that you are planning to test.

TESTING CLAIMS ABOUT 2 MEANS

In this section we will be testing a claim about two means (that the mean of one group is less than, greater than, or equal to the mean of another group). You will first need to determine if the groups are **dependent,** i.e., the values in one sample are related to the values in another sample, e.g., before and after tests, or tests on spouses or if the groups are **independent,** i.e., the values in one sample are not related to the values in another sample.

If you can answer yes to one of the questions below, you can use the identical statistical test described in this section. Are you claiming that:

____1.   One product, program, or treatment is

better than another?

____2. One group is better (or worse) than another? (with respect to some variable).

Many real and practical situations involve testing hypotheses made about two population means. For example, an educator may want to compare mean test scores produced by two different teaching methods to see if they are the same. A nutritionist might wish to compare the weight loss that results from patients on two different diet plans to determine which one is more effective. A psychologist may want to test for a difference in mean reaction times between men and women to determine if women respond more quickly than men in an emergency situation.

If your two samples (groups) are dependent, i.e., the values in one sample are related to the values in the other in some way, a t-statistic is computed and a simple **paired t test** may be used to test your claim. This **t** statistic is obtained by computing the differences between the related means and then obtaining the mean of all these differences.

If your two samples are independent, ,i.e. the values in one sample are not related to the values in the other, and the size of each group (n) is 30 or more, *or* you know the standard deviations of the population, then a simple **Z** statistic may be computed and a **paired Z-test** could be ordered. In this case, the differences in the population means are computed,.and subtracted from the differences in the sample means. The result is divided by the square root of the sum of each variance divided by the respective sample size.

BUT if the two samples are independent, the sample size (n) is not greater than or equal to 30 for each group, and the population standard deviation is not known, then who do you call? The **F (team) test**. the F test is used first to see if the standard deviations are equal (relatively small **f** value indicates that the standard deviations are the same). If the **f** value is "relatively" small, then you, or preferably your computer, would need to perform a **t** test to test your hypothesis. This involves a very tedious computation. However, if the **f** test was to yield a "relatively" large F value, this would lead to a more benign **t** test .

Once the mean and standard deviation are computed for each sample, it is customary to identify the group with the larger standard deviation as group 1 and the other sample as group 2.

The non-parametric counterpart of the paired **Z** or **T**-test is: the **Wilcoxon signed-ranks test** if samples are dependent and **Wilcoxon Rank-Sum Test** if samples are independent.

TESTING CLAIMS ABOUT 3 OR MORE MEANS

If you can answer yes to one of the questions below, you can use the identical statistical test described in this section. Are you claiming that:

___1.   There is a difference between three or more products, programs, or treatments?

___2.   There is a different outcome from the same program, product or treatment amongst three or more different groups?

Claims about three or more means require the creation of an f-statistic, and the performing of an **F test** is on the menu. Here you, or hopefully your computer, will compare the <u>variances</u> between the samples to the <u>variances</u> within the samples. The nickname for what's happening here is **ANOVA** (Analysis of Variance). It is an extension of the **t** test used for testing two means. The null hypothesis is that the means are equal.

An **F** value close to 1 would indicate that there are no significant differences between the sample means. A "relatively large" **F** value will cause you to reject the null hypothesis and conclude that the means in the samples are not equal. Some important things to know about the F distribution:

1. It is not symmetric, but rather, it is skewed to the right.

2. The values of F can be 0 or positive, but not negative.

3. There is a different F distribuiton for each pair of degrees of freedom for the numerator and denominator.

Note: If you are asking yourself or the Dissertation Cookbook: "Why are we dealing with variances when the claim is about means?" you would be asking a very good question. The answer is that the variance, or the standard deviation squared, is determined by, and dependent on, the mean, so it is actually all in the family!

FOR YOUR INFORMATION AND EDUCATION:

The method of ANOVA owes its beginning to Sir Ronald A. Fisher (1890-1962) and received its early impetus because of its applications to problems in agricultural research. It is such a powerful statistical tool that it has since found applications in just about every branch of scientific research, including economics, psychology, marketing research, and industrial engineering, to mention just a few.

The following example will be testing a claim about three means obtained from a sample Using the "sss candoall" model. A report on the findings follows the example.

Example: A study was done to investigate the time in minutes for police from three precincts to arrive at the scene of a crime. Sample results from similar types of crimes are:

A: 7   4   4   3
      sample size: $n = 4$, mean. $x = 4.5$, variance, $s^2 = 3.0$
B: 9   5   7
      sample size: $n = 3$, mean $x = 7.0$, variance, $s^2 = 4.2$
C: 2   3   5   3   8
      sample size: $n = 5$, mean $x = 4.2$, variance, $s^2 = 5.7$

At the 0.05 significance level, test the claim that the precincts have the same mean reaction time to similar crimes.

What are the three s's?

(a) What is the **S**ubstantive hypothesis?
      [What does the researcher think will happen?]
   The reaction times are similar in the three precincts.

(b) How large is the **S**ample size that was studied?
   The three groups have sample sizes of 4, 3, and 5, respectively.

(c) What descriptive **S**tatistic was determined by the sample?
   The means and variances for each group were determined.

Now we are ready to take the information obtained in (a), (b), and (c) and employ the eight step CANDOALL recipe to test this hypothesis.

We will determine if the claim; *The reaction times are similar* is statistically correct.

1.   Identify the Claim (C) to be tested and express it in symbolic   form.

$$\mu_a = \mu_b = \mu_c$$

That is, there is a claim that the mean reaction time in each precinct is the same

2.   Express in symbolic form the Alternative (A) statement that would be true if the original claim is false.

$$\mu_a \neq \mu_b \neq \mu_c$$

Remember we must cover all possibilities

3.   Identify the Null (N) and alternative hypothesis.

Note: The null hypothesis should be the one that contains *no change* (an equal sign).

$H_0: \mu_a = \mu_b = \mu_c$ (Null hypothesis)
$H_1: \mu_a \neq \mu_b \neq \mu_c$ (Alternative hypothesis)

Remember: A statistical test is designed to <u>accept</u> or <u>reject</u> (i.e., fail to accept) the statistical **null hypothesis** being examined.

4. Decide (D) on the level of significance, alpha (α), based on the seriousness of a *type I error*

Note: This is the mistake of rejecting the null hypothesis when it is in fact true. Make alpha small if the consequences of rejecting a true alpha are severe. The smaller the alpha value, the less likely you will be to reject the null hypothesis. Alpha values 0.05 and 0.01 are very common.

$$\alpha = 0.05$$

5. Order (O) a statistical test and sampling distribution that is relevant to the study.* (see Table 1)

Since the claim involves data from three groups and we wish to test the hypothesis that the differences among the sample means is due to chance, we can use the ANOVA test.

Note: The following assumptions apply when using the ANOVA: The population has a normal distributio; the populations have the same variance (or standard deviation); the sampes are random and independent of each other.

6. Perform the Arithmetic (A) and determine: the test statistic, the critical value, and the critical region.

Note: It would be best to let the computer or a calculator assist you on this.

To perform an ANOVA test we need to compute:
The number of samples, k,
$$k = 3$$
The mean of all the times, x
$$x = 5.0$$
The variance between the samples (vbs)
this is found by subtracting the mean (5.0) from the variance of each sample, squaring the differences, then multiplying each by the sample size and finally adding up the results for each sample.
$$vbs = 8.123$$
The variance within the samples (vws)
this is found by multiplying the variance of each sample by one less than the number in the sample, adding the results (this equals 39.8), and then dividing by the total population minus the number of samples, 9.
$$vws = 4.4222$$

The test statistic is F = <u>variance between samples</u>
                                  variance within samples
$$F = 1.8317$$

The   degrees of freedom in the numerator
$$k-1 = 3-1 = 2.$$
The degrees of freedom in the denominator
$$n-k = 12-3 = 9.$$

Note: <u>Degrees of freedom</u> is the number of values that are free to vary after certain restrictions have been imposed on all values. For example, if 10 scores must total 80, then we can freely assign values to the first 9 scores, but the tenth score would then be determined so that there would be 9 degrees of freedom. In a test using an F statistic we need to find the degrees of freedom in both the numerator and the denominator.

The critical value of f = 4.2565 (this can be found on a table or from a computer program).

7. Look (L) to accept or reject the null hypothesis.

Note: This is a right-tailed test since the F statistic yields only positive values.

Since the test statistic of f = 1.8317 does not exceed the critical value of F = 4.2565, we fail to reject the null hypothesis that the means are equal.

Note: The shape of an F distribution is slightly different for each sample size n. The $\alpha = 0.05$ level employs us to find an F value that will separate the curve into 2 unequal regions; the smaller one with an area of **0.05** (5%), and the larger one with an area of 100%- 5% or 95% (often referred to as a 95% confidence level).

8. In Lay terms (L) write what happened.
There is insufficient sample evidence to warrant rejection of the claim that the means are equal.

Note: In order for statistics to make sense in research it is important to use a rigorously controlled design in which other factors are forced to be constant.   The design of the experiment is critically important, and no statistical calisthenics can salvage a poor design.

Writing About This Study in a Research Paper

If this study were to be published in a research journal, or was part of a master thesis or doctoral dissertation, the following *script* could be used to summarize the statistical findings. This information usually appears in the data analysis section of a document but could also be properly placed in the section where the conclusion of the study is found, or even in the methodology section of the paper. This information would also be very appropriate to place in the abstract of the study.

A study was conducted to investigate the time in minutes for police from three precincts to arrive at the scene of a crime. Sample results from similar types of crimes were found to be:

A: 7   4   4   3
      sample size: n = 4, mean, x, = 4.5, variance, s^2 = 3.0
B: 9   5   7
      sample size: n = 3, mean, x = 7.0, variance, s^2 = 4.2
C: 2   3   5   3   8
      sample size: n = 5, mean, x = 4.2 variance, s^2 = 5.7

At the α =0.05 significance level, the claim that the precincts had the same mean reaction time to similar crimes was tested. The null hypothesis is the claim that the samples come from populations with the same mean:

H_0: $\mu_A = \mu_B = \mu_C$, and the alternative Hypothesis is , H_1: $\mu_A \neq \mu_B \neq \mu_C$.

To determine if there are any statistically significant differences between the means of the three groups, an ANOVA test was performed. An F distribution was employed to compare the two different estimates of the variance common to the different groups (i.e., variation between samples, and variation within the samples). A test statistic of f = 1.8317 was obtained. With 2 degrees of freedom for the numerator and 9 degrees of freedom for the denominator, the critical f value of 4.2565 was determined. Since the test-f does not exceed the critical-f value, the null hypothesis was not rejected. There is insufficient sample evidence to reject the claim that the mean values were equal.

The non-parametric counterpart of ANOVA is: the **Kruskal-Wallis Test.**

TESTING A CLAIM ABOUT
PROPORTIONS/PERCENTAGES

If you can answer yes to one of the questions below, you can use the identical statistical test described in this section. Are you claiming that:

___1. A certain percent or ratio is higher or lower than what is believed?

___2. There is a characteristic of a group that
is actually prevalent in a higher or lower percent

Data at the nominal (name only) level of measurement
lacks any real numerical significance and is essentially
qualitative in nature. One way to make a quantitative
analysis using qualitative data is to represent that data in
the form of a percentage or a ratio. This representation is
very useful in a variety of applications, including surveys,
polls, and quality control considerations involving the
percentage of defective parts.

A **Z test** will work fine here provided that the size of
your population is large enough.* The test statistic is:

$$z = \frac{p - p'}{\sqrt{pq/n}}$$

where n = sample size, p = population proportion (which appears in
the null hypothesis), q = 1- p, and p' is the proportion computed
from the sample.

Note: The p in the formula is different from the "p" value we use to determine
significance in hypothesis testing. It is important to be aware that in mathematics
oftentimes the same symbol can have more than one interpretation. While doing
mathematics keep this in mind and remember to learn the meaning of a symbol in
its context.

Example: If an administrator believes that less than 48%
of the teachers in a school district support the districts
discipline policy, the claim can be checked based on the
response of a random sample of teachers.
If 720 teachers were sampled and 54.2% actually favored
stricter discipline, then to check the administrator's claim,
we would use: p' = .542, n =720, p = .48, q =.52, and

$$z = (0.542-0.48)/\sqrt{(0.48 \times 0.52)/720} = 3.33$$

Since np > 5 and nq > 5, then your population is large enough.

Note: If the percent (p), you are testing is 80%, 100% - p = 20% which is q. To
qualify for this test your population would need to be larger than 25 since 25
(0.20) = 5.

TESTING CLAIMS ABOUT
STANDARD DEVIATIONS AND VARIABILITY

Many real and practical situations demand decisions or inferences about **variances** and **standard deviations**. In manufacturing, quality control engineers want to ensure that a product is on the average acceptable but also want to produce items of consistent quality so there are as few defects as possible. Consistency is measured by variances.

FOR YOUR INFORMATION AND EDUCATION:

During World War II, 35,000 American engineers and technicians were taught to use statistics to improve the quality of war material through the efforts of Dr. W. Edwards Deming (born in Sioux City, Iowa, on October 14, 1900). Deming's work was brought to the attention of the Union of Japanese Scientists and Engineers (JUSE). JUSE called upon Deming to help its members increase productivity. The Japanese people were convinced by Deming that quality drives profits up The rebirth of Japanese industry and its worldwide success is attributed to the ideas and the teachings of Deming. In gratitude, Deming was awarded Japan's Second Order Medal of the Sacred Treasure by the late Emperor Hirohito.

If you can answer yes to one of the questions below, you can use the identical statistical test described in this section. Are you claiming that:

___1. a product, program, or treatment has more or less variability than the standard?

___2. a product, program, or treatment is more or less consistent than the standard?

To test claims involving variability, the researcher usually turns to a **Chi-square** statistic.

FOR YOUR INFORMATION AND EDUCATION:

Both the **t and Chi square (X^2)** distributions have a slightly different shape depending on n, the number in the sample. For this reason, you need to determine the "**degrees of freedom**" to find out what shape curve will be used to obtain the test statistics.

The "degrees of freedom" refer to the number of observations or scores minus the number of parameters that are being studied. (Informally, it is the number of times you can miss a certain targeted number and still have a chance of obtaining that desired outcome). When you use a sample size of (n) to investigate (1) parameter, e.g., a mean or standard deviation, the degrees of freedom are: (n-1), when investigating a relationship between **2** variables then the degrees of freedom are: (n-2)

The test statistics used in tests of hypotheses involving variances or standard deviations, is **chi-square**, x^2, where:

$$x^2 = \frac{(n-1)\ s^2}{\partial^2}$$

n = sample size, s^2 is the sample variance and the population variance is ∂^2.

Example: A supermarket finds that the average check out waiting time for a customer on Saturday mornings is 8 minutes with a standard deviation of 6.2 minutes. One Saturday management experimented with a single main waiting time. They sampled 25 customers and found that the average waiting time remained 8 minutes, but the standard deviation went down to 3.8 minutes. Test the claim that the single line causes lower variation in waiting time.

Here the statistic x^2 can be used to test the claim.

$$x^2 = \frac{(25-1)(3.8)^2}{(6.2)^2} = 9.016$$

There would be 24 degrees of freedom in this problem since n = 25

TESTING A CLAIM ABOUT THE RELATION BETWEEN TWO VARIABLES
(CORRELATION AND REGRESSION ANALYSIS)

Many real and practical situations demand decisions or inferences about how data from a certain variable can be used to determine the value of some other related variable. For example, a Florida study of the number of powerboat registrations and the number of accidental manatee deaths confirmed that there was a significant positive correlation. As a result, Florida created coastal sanctuaries where powerboats are prohibited so that manatees could thrive. A study in Sweden found that there was a higher incidence of leukemia among children who lived within 300 meters of a high-tension power line during a 25-year period. This led Sweden's government to consider regulations that would reduce housing in close proximity to high-tension power lines.

If you are analyzing the strength of a relationship between paired data or **bivariate data,** and you can answer yes to the questions below, you can use the identical statistical test described in this section. Are you claiming that:

___1.   There is a relationship or correlation between two factors, two events or two characteristics?

In regression and correlation analysis you usually:

1.   Record the information in table form.

2.   Draw a **scatter diagram** to see any "obvious" relationship or trends.

3.   Compute the **correlation coefficient, r** (rho) aka the Pearson Correlation Coefficient factor, to obtain objective analysis that will uncover the magnitude and significance of the relationship between the variables.

4. Determine if **r** is statistically significant.

5. If **r** is statistically significant then you can use **regression analysis** to determine what the relationship between the variables is.

Example: Suppose randomly selected students are given a standard I.Q. test and then tested for their levels of math anxiety using a MARS (math anxiety rating scale) test:

1.   Record information in table form:

IQ (I)	103	113	119	107	78	153	111	128	135	86
MARS (M)	75	68	65	70	86	21	85	45	24	73

The researcher's hypothesis is that students with higher IQ's have lower levels of math anxiety. [Note: The independent variable is IQ scores which are being used to predict the dependent variable MARS scores].

Ho: **r** = 0 (there is no relationship)
H1: **r** ≠ 0 (there is a relationship)

Note: These will usually be the hypotheses in regression analysis.

2.   Draw a scatter diagram:

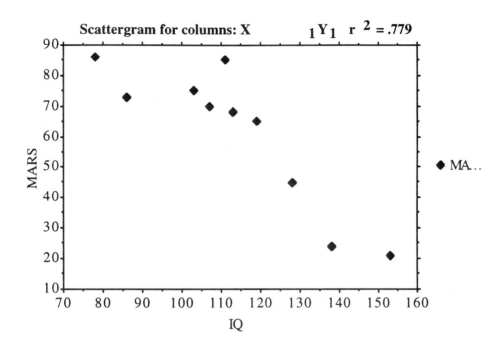

Scattergram for columns: X $_1$Y$_1$ r^2 = .779

The points in the figure above seem to follow a downward pattern, so we might conclude that there *is* a relationship between IQ and levels of Math anxiety, but this is somewhat subjective.

3. Compute **r**

To obtain a more precise and objective analysis we can compute the linear coefficient constant, r. Computing **r** is a tedious exercise in arithmetic but practically any statistical computer program or scientific calculator would willingly help you along. In our example the very friendly program STATVIEW was used to determine our **r** = -.882

Corr. Coeff. X $_1$: IQ   Y $_1$: MARS

Count:	Covariance:	Correlation:	R-squared:
10	-464.8	-.882	.779

Some of the properties or this number **r** are:

1. The computed value of **r** must be between (-1) and (+1). (If it's not then someone or something messed up.)

2. A strong positive correlation would yield an r value close to (+1), a strong negative linear correlation would be close to (-1).

3. If **r** is close to 0 we conclude that there is no significant linear correlation between (X) and (Y).

Checking the table, we find that with a sample size of 10, (n = 10), the value **r** = -.882 indicating a strong negative correlation between measures of IQ and measures of math anxiety levels. The **r-squared** number (0.779) indicates that 77.9% of a person's MARS score could be explained by a person's I.Q..

4. If there is a significant relation, then regression analysis is used to determine what that relationship is. If the relation is linear, the equation of the line of best fit can be determined. [For 2 variables, the equation of a line can be expressed as y = mx + b, where *m* is the slope and *b* is the *y* intercept]

Simple Regression X $_1$: IQ   Y $_1$: MARS

Beta Coefficient Table

Variable:	Coefficient:	Std. Err.:	Std. Coeff.:	t-Value:	Probability:
INTERCEPT	165.04				
SLOPE	-.914	.172	-.882	5.303	.0007

Confidence Intervals Table

Variable:	95% Lower:	95% Upper:	90% Lower:	90% Upper:
MEAN (X,Y)	52.696	69.704	54.342	68.058
SLOPE	-1.312	-.517	-1.235	-.594

Residual : Column 6 Std. Residual : Column 7 Fitted : Column 8 Predicted : Column 9

Thus, the equation of the line of best fit for Y = Mars test, and X = I.Q., would be

Y = -.914 **X** + 165.04

The non-parametric counterpart to **r** is: the **Spearman's rank correlation coefficient (r$_s$) or r.**

cutting board:

How alike are two peoples' tastes in television shows? The following activity will employ the nonparametric, Spearman rank correlation coefficient test to help determine the answer to this question. You will need a friend or a relative to do this activity.

1. In Column I of the chart provided in step (3), list 10 different TV shows that you and a friend or relative are familiar with. Try to have at least one news show, a situation comedy, a mystery, a variety show, a talk show, and a drama. Include shows that you like as well as those that you dislike.

2. In column II, rank the shows that are listed where 1 is your favorite (the one you would be most inclined to watch) and 10 is your least favorite (the one you would be least inclined to watch).

3. Have your friend or relative do a similar ranking in column III.

	I TV Shows	II Your Ratings	III F/R Ratings	IV d	V d^2
A.	ER	9	6	3	9
B.	ESPN	10	9	1	1
C.	Law + order	8	2	6	36
D.	Friends	7	1	6	36
E.	Bev Hills 90210	6	7	-1	1
F.	clasic movies	1	3	-2	4
G.	Date line	5	4	1	1
H.	oprah	4	8	-4	16
I.	Simpsons	3	5	-2	4
J.	MTV	2	10	-8	16

124

3. Use the graph on the right to plot the ordered pairs consisting of the two rankings. Label the points with the letters corresponding to the shows in the list.   If the two rankings were identical, the points would be on a starting line pointing Northeast and forming a 45 degree angle with both axis. If you were in total disagreement then the points would be on a straight line pointing Southeast and also from a 45 degree angle with both axes.

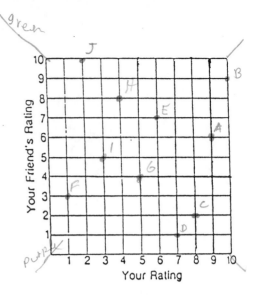

4. Although the scattergram you created in step (3) might give you an impression of how the two ratings match or correlate with each other, it is probably not very definitive. To determine "how closely correlated" these rankings are, we can use the **r statistics** and the Spearman rank correlation coefficient which we will compute in steps (5) , (6) and (7).

5. Go back to the chart in step (2) and compute d, the difference between the two ratings for each show, and d^2 that is (d)(d). After you have all the d^2 add them up.

6. The formula for finding the rank correlation is:

$$r_s = 1 - \frac{6\Sigma d^2}{n(n^2 - 1)}$$

$6(124) = \frac{744}{990}$

$1 - \frac{744}{990}$

7. To do this on your calculator, multiply the sum of your d^2 numbers by 6. Divide this product by 990 which is the denominator, (10)(99). Store this number in memory +. Compute 1 minus memory recall. The number in the display is your **r** number. It should be between -1 and +1.

8. The table on the right indicates that for your sample size of 10, an **r** value of 0.564 or greater would indicate a positive correlation with an alpha of 0.10, (a negative value less than - 0.564 would indicate a negative correlation with an alpha value of 0.10). The closer **r** is to 1 or -1, the stronger the relation. An **r** value close to 0 indicates no particular relation. What can you conclude from this test? Should you and this other person turn on the tube when you are together or would it be better to find a different activity?

Critical Values of Spearman's Rank Correlation Coefficient r_s

n	$\alpha = 0.10$	$\alpha = 0.05$	$\alpha = 0.02$	$\alpha = 0.01$
5	.900	—	—	—
6	.829	.886	.943	—
7	.714	.786	.893	—
8	.643	.738	.833	.881
9	.600	.683	.783	.833
10	.564	.648	.745	.794
11	.523	.623	.736	.818
12	.497	.591	.703	.780
13	.475	.566	.673	.745
14	.457	.545	.646	.716
15	.441	.525	.623	.689
16	.425	.507	.601	.666
17	.412	.490	.582	.645
18	.399	.476	.564	.625
19	.388	.462	.549	.608
20	.377	.450	.534	.591

More on Correlational Statistics
Warning: Correlation does not imply CAUSATION!

The Purpose of **Correlational Research** is to find *Co-relationships* between two or more variables with the hope of better understanding the conditions and events we encounter and with the hope of making predictions about the future. [From the Annals of Chaos Theory: *Predictions are usually very difficult-- especially if they are about the future; predictions are like diapers, both need to be changed often and for the same reason!*].

As was noted previously, the linear correlation coefficient, r, measures the strength of the linear relationship between two paired variables in a sample. If there is a linear correlation, that is, if r is "large enough," between two variables, then regression analysis is used to identify the relationship with the hope of predicting one variable from the other.

Note: If there is no significant linear correlation, then a regression equation cannot be used to make predictions.

A regression equation based on old data is not necessarily valid now. The regression equation relating used car prices and ages of cars is no longer usable if it is based on data from the 1960s. Often a scattergram is plotted to get a visual view of the correlation and possible regression equation.

Note: Nonlinear relationships can also be determined, but because more complex mathematics are used to describe and interpret data, they are used considerably less often. The following are characteristics of all linear correlational studies:

1. Main research questions are stated as null hypotheses, i.e., "no" relationship exists between the variables being studied.

2. In simple correlation, there are two measures for each individual in the sample.

3. To apply parametric methods, there must be at least 30 individuals in the study.

4. Can be used to measure "the degree" of relationships, not simply whether a relationship exists.

5. A perfect positive correlation is 1.00; a perfect negative (inverse) is -1.00.

6. A correlation of 0 indicates no linear relationship exists.

7. If when two variables, x and y, are correlated so that $r = .5$, then we say that $(0.5)^2$ or 0.25 or 25% of their variation is common, or variable x can predict 25% of the variance in y.

The Pearson Product Moment Correlation Coefficient (that is a mouthful!) or simply the Pearson r, is the most common measure of the strength of the linear relationship between two variables. It is named for Karl Pearson (1857-1936) who originally developed it. The Spearman Rank Correlation Coefficient, or Spearman r, (which we performed above), used for ranked data or when you have a sample size less than 30 ($n<30$), is the second most popular measure of the strength of the linear relationship between two variables. To measure the strength of the linear relationship between test items for reliability purposes, the Cronbach alpha is the most efficient method of measuring the internal consistency.

Both the Spearman and Pearson tests are examples of **bivariate correlation** -- tests where only two variables are being investigated. The table (2) helps us determine when these statistical tests, and others, can be used to determine correlation and regression based on the type of data collected.

Note: The following definitions are used in the table (2):

   Continuous scores: Scores can be measured using a rational scale.
   Ranked data: Likert-type Scale, class Rankings
   Dichotomy: subjects classified into two categories-- Republican V. Democrat
   Artificial: pass V. fail (arbitrary decision); true dichotomy (male V. female).

Table (2)

Technique	Symbol	Variable 1	Variable 2	Remarks
Pearson	r	Continuous	Continuous	Smallest standard of error
Spearman Rank	r	Ranks	Ranks	Used also when n< 30
Kendall's tau	t	Ranks	Ranks	Used for n < 10
Biserial Correlation (Cronbach)	a/bis	Artificial Dichotomy	Continuous	Sometimes exceeds 1 often used in item analysis.
Widespread biserial correlation	r/wbis	Artificial Dichotomy	Continuous	Looking for extremes on Variable 1
Point- biserial correlation	r/pbis	True Dichotomy	Continuous	Yields lower correlation than r/biserial
Tetrachoric correlation	r/t	Artificial Dichotomy	Artificial Dichotomy	Used when Var 1 and 2 can be split arbitrarily
Phi coefficient	f	True Dichotomy	True Dichotomy	
Correlation ratio eta	h	Continuous	Continuous	Nonlinear Relationships

Multivariate Correlational statistics

If you wish to test a claim that multiple independent variables might be used to make a prediction about a dependent variable, you have several possible tests that can be constructed. Such studies involve **Multivariate Correlational Statistics**

Discriminate Analysis -- Used to determine the correlation between two or more predictor variables and a dichotomous criterion variable. The main use of discriminant analysis is to predict group membership (e.g., success/non-success) from a set of predictors. If a set of variables is found which provide satisfactory discrimination, classification equations can be derived, their use checked out through hit/rate tables, and if good, they can be used to classify new subjects who were not in the original analysis. In order to use discriminate analysis certain assumptions (conditions) must be met:

* At least 2 x number of subjects as variables in study.
* Each groups has at least n = # of variables.
* Groups have the same variance/covariance structures.
* All variables are normally distributed.

Canonical Correlation -- Used to predict a combination of several criterion variables from a combination of several predictor variables.

Path Analysis-- Used to test theories about hypothesized causal links between variables that are correlated.

Factor Analysis -- Used to reduce a large number of variables to a few factors by combining variables that are moderately or highly correlated with one another.

Differential Analysis -- Used to examine correlation between variables among homogeneous subgroups within a sample; can be used to identify moderator variables that improve a measure's predictive validity.

Multiple Regression -- Used to determine the correlation between a criterion variable and a combination of two or more predictor variables. As in any regression method we need the following conditions to be met: We are investigating linear relationships; for each x value, y is a random variable having a normal distribution. All of the y variables have the same variance; for a given value of x, the distribution of y values has a mean that lies on the regression line.

Note: Results are not seriously affected if departures from normal distributions and equal variances are not too extreme.

The following example illustrates how a researcher might use different multivariate correlational statistics in a research project.

Example: Suppose a researcher has, among other data, scores on three measures for a group of teachers working overseas:

1. years of experience as a teacher
2. extent of travel while growing up
3. tolerance for ambiguity.

Research Question: *Can these measures (or other factors) predict the degree of adaptation to the overseas culture they are working in?*

Discriminate Analysis: Hypothesis (1): The outcome is dichotomous between those who adapted well and those who adapted poorly based on these three measures. Hypothesis (2): Knowing these three factors could be used to predict success.

Multiple Regression: Hypothesis: Some combination of the three predictor measures correlates better with predicting the outcome measure than any one predictor alone.

Canonical Correlation: Hypothesis: several measures of adaptation could be quantified, i.e., adaptation to food, climate, customs, etc. based on these predictors.

Path Analysis: Hypothesis: Childhood travel experience leads to tolerance for ambiguity and desire for travel as an adult, and this makes it more likely that teachers will score high on these predictors which will lead them to seek an overseas teaching experience and adapt well to the experience.

Factor Analysis: Suppose there are five more (a total of eight) adaptive measures which could be determined. All eight measures can be examined to determine whether they cluster into groups such as: education, experience, personality traits, etc.

ANALYSIS OF COVARIANCE

A "yes" on question one below will lead you to a different type of statistical test involving bivariate data. Are you claiming that:

___1. Two groups being compared come from the same population and contain similar characteristics?

If you are planning to divide your subjects into two groups (perhaps a control group and an experimental group), or if you are planning to use two different treatments on two different groups, then problems in randomization and matching the groups might be a concern.

A relatively new statistical process called *analysis of covariance* (**ANCOVA**) has been developed to equate the groups on certain relevant variables identified prior to the investigation. Pre-test mean scores are often used as covariates.

The following guidelines should be used in the analysis of covariance:

1. The correlation of the covariate (some variable different than the one you are testing) and the response variable should be statistically and educationally significant.

2. The covariate should have a high reliability.

3. The covariate should be a variable that is measured prior to any portion of the treatments.

4. The conditions of homogeneity of regression should be met. The slopes of the regression lines describing the linear relationships of the criterion variable and the covariate from cell to cell must not be statistically different.

5. All follow-up procedures for significant interaction or "post-hoc comparisons" should be made with the adjusted cell or adjusted marginal means.

ANCOVA is a transformation from raw scores to adjusted scores which take into account the effects of the covariate. ANCOVA allows us to compensate somewhat when groups are selected by non random methods

The non-parametric counterpart of ANCOVA is the **Runs Test.**

If your hypothesis is that many variables or factors are contributing to a certain condition, you may wish to use **multiple regression analysis.** This is similar to linear regression analysis with a significant increase in number crunching. If this is not how you wish to spend several hours of your day, we recommend that you employ a computer to crank out the numerical information necessary to use multiple regression analysis.

CONTINGENCY TABLES:

If you only want to test:

___1. Whether or not two variables are dependent on one another, (e.g., are death and smoking dependent variables; are SAT scores and high school grades independent variables?)

you might consider using a **contingency table.**

The null hypothesis would be that the variables are independent. Setting up a contingency table is easy; the rows are one variable, the columns another. In contingency table analysis you determine how closely the amount in each cell coincides with the expected value of each cell if the two variables were independent.

The following contingency table lists the response to a bill pertaining to gun control.

	In favor	Opposed
Northeast	10	30
Southeast	15	25
Northwest	35	10
Southwest	10	25

Notice that cell 1 indicates that 10 people in the Northeast were in favor of the bill.

Example: In the previous contingency table, 40 out of 160 (1/4) of those surveyed were from the Northeast. If the two variables were independent, you would expect 1/2 of that amount (20) to be in favor of the amendment since there were only two choices.

To determine how close the expected values are to the actual values, the test statistic **chi-square** is determined. Small values of chi-square support the claim of independence between the two variables. That is, chi-square will be small when observed and expected frequencies are close. Large values of chi-square would cause the null hypothesis to be rejected and reflect significant differences between observed and expected frequencies.

Before you move into your final PHASE, use the cutting board below to assist you in deciding what spices you can use in yout study. To further assist you, a glossary of statistical terms has been provided for you.

cutting board:

1. Underline the terms that best complete the sentence. I will be testing a claim about:

a mean, a standard deviation, a proportion, (2) means, (2) variances, a relationship between (2) variables, the independence of (2) variables, relationship between more than (2) variables.

2. If you will be using non-parametric testing, underline the test(s) that you will use:

Sign Test, Wilcoxon Signed-Ranks, Wilcoxon Rank-Sum Test, Kruskal-Wallis Test, Spearman Rank Correlation, Runs Test

3. If you plan to use parametric testing, underline the statistic(s) that you plan to use:

Z-test, **T**-test, paired **t** or **z** test, **X²**, **r**, **F**-test

4. Why did you choose the statistic(s) in (2) and/or (3)? _____

_____

5. After your data are collected, make sure you sojourn this section again and fill out all information which is relevant to your research study. Once this is accomplished, You will be able to "fly" through Chapter 4 of your dissertation.

Statistical Terms

One of the keys to understanding a specialized field is getting to know its jargon, its technical vocabulary. As you continue to put together your research project you might come across words that you are unfamiliar with. The following words often appear in quantitative studies. Remember to refer to them as needed.

Alternative Hypothesis: The hypothesis that would be accepted if the null hypothesis is not accepted.

Analysis of Variance (ANOVA): A statistical method for determining the significance of the differences among a set of sample means.

The Dissertation Cookbook   133

Central Limit Theorem: A mathematical conjecture that informs us that the sampling distribution of the mean approaches a normal curve as the sample size, n, gets larger.

Chi-square Distribution: A continuous probability distribution that could be used to test hypotheses involving variation.

Confidence Interval: A range of values used to estimate some population parameter with a specific level of confidence. In most statistical tests, confidence levels are between 95% and 99%.

Correlation: A relationship between variables such that increases or decreases in the value of one variable tend to be accompanied by increases or decreases in the other.

Correlation Coefficient: A measurement between -1 and 1 indicating the strength of the relationship between two variables.

Critical Region: The area of the sampling distribution that covers the value of the test statistic that are not due to chance variation. In most tests it represents between 1% and 5% of the graph of the distribution.

Critical Value: The value from a sampling distribution which separates chance variations from variations that not due to chance.

Data: Facts and figures collected through research.

Dependent Variable: The variable that is measured and analyzed in an experiment. In traditional algebra, in equations of the form $y =$___ $x +$ ____, it is usually agreed that y is the dependent variable.

Dependent Samples: The values in one sample are related to the values in another sample. Before and after results are dependent samples.

Descriptive Statistics: The methods used to summarize the key characteristics of known population and sample data.

Degrees of Freedom: The number of values that are free to vary after certain restrictions have been imposed on all values.

Experiment: Process that allows observations to be made. In probability an experiment can be repeated over and over again under the same conditions.

F Distribution: A continuous probability distribution used in tests comparing two variances.

Goodness of Fit: Degree to which observed data coincide with theoretical expectations.

Histogram: A graph of connected vertical rectangles representing the frequency distribution of a set of data.

Hypothesis: A statement or claim that some characteristic of a population is true.

Hypothesis Test: A method for testing claims made about populations. Also called test of significance. In this tutorial the CANDOALL method is used to test hypotheses.

Independent Variable: The treatment variable. In traditional algebra, in equations of the form y =___ x + ____, it is usually agreed that x is the independent variable.

Inferential Statistics: The methods of using sample data to make generalizations or inferences about a population.

Interval Scale: A measurement scale in which equal differences between numbers stand for equal differences in the thing measured. The zero point is arbitrarily defined. Temperature is measured on an interval scale.

Kruskal-Wallis Test: A nonparametric hypothesis test used to compare three or more independent samples.

Left-tail test: Hypothesis test in which the critical region is located in the extreme left area of the probability distribution. The alternative hypothesis is the claim that a quantity is less than a certain value.

Level of Significance: The probability level at which then null hypothesis is rejected. Usually represented by the Greek letter alpha (α).

Mean: A measure of central tendency, the arithmetic average; the sum of scores divided by the number of scores.

Median: A measure of central tendency which divides a distribution of scores into two equal halves so that half the scores are above the median and half are below it.

Mode: A measure of central tendency that represents the most fashionable, or most frequently occurring score.

Multiple Regression: Study of linear relationships among three or more variables.

Nominal Data: Data that consists of names only; no real quantitative value. Often numbers are arbitrarily assigned to nominal data, such as Male = 0, Female = 1.

Nonparametric Statistical Methods: Statistical methods that do not require a normal distribution or that data be interval or rational.

Normal Distribution: (Gaussian Curve) A theoretical bell-shaped, symmetrical, distribution based on frequency of occurrence of chance events.

Null Hypothesis: The assumption of no change; the difference between an observed statistic and a proposed parameter is the result of chance.

Odds in Favor: The number of ways an event can happen compared to the number of ways that it cannot happen.

Ogive: A graphical method of representing cumulative frequencies.

One-Tailed Test: A statistical test in which the critical region lies in one tail of the distribution.

One-way Analysis of Variance: Analysis of variance involving data classified into groups according to a single criterion.

Ordinal Scale: A rank-ordered scale of measurement in which equal differences between numbers do not represent equal differences between the thing measured. The Likert-type scale is a common ordinal scale.

Parameter: Some numerical characteristic of a population.

Parametric Methods: Statistical procedures for testing hypotheses or estimating parameters based on population parameters that are measured on interval or rational scores. Data is usually normally distributed.

Pie Chart: Graphical method of representing data in the form of a circle containing wedges.

Population: All members of a specified group.

Probability: A measure of the likelihood that a given event will occur. Mathematical probabilities are expressed as numbers between 0 and 1.

Probability Distribution: Collection of values of a random variable along with their corresponding probabilities.

P-Value: The probability that a test statistic in a hypothesis test is at least as extreme as the one actually obtained. A p value is found after a test statistic is determined. It indicates how likely the results of an experiment was due to a chance happening.

Qualitative Variable: A variable that is often measured with nominal data.

Quantitative Variable: A variable that is measured with interval and rational data.

Random Sample: A subset of a population chosen in such away that any member of the population has an equal chance of being selected.

Range: The difference between the highest and lowest score.

Ratio Scale: A scale that has equal differences and equal ratios between values, and a true zero point. Heights, weights, and time are measured on rational scales.

Raw Score: A score obtained in an experiment which has not been organized or analyzed.

Regression Line: The line of best fit that runs through a scatterplot.

Right Tailed Test: Hypothesis test in which the critical region is located in the extreme right area of the probability distribution. The alternative hypothesis is the claim that a quantity is greater than a certain value.

Sample: A subset of a population.

Sampling Error: Errors resulting from the sampling process itself.

Scattergram: The points that results when a distribution of paired values is plotted on a graph.

Sign Test: A nonparametric hypothesis test used to compare samples from two populations.

Significance Level: The probability that serves as a cutoff between results attributed to chance happenings and results attributed to significant differences.

Skewed Distribution: An asymmetrical distribution.

Spearman's Rank Correlation Coefficient: Measure of the strength of the relationship between two variables.

Spearman's Rho: A correlation statistic for two sets of ranked data.

Standard Deviation: The "weighted" average amount that individual scores deviate from the mean of a distribution of scores. A measure of dispersion equal to the square root of the variance. At least 75% of all scores will fall within the interval from two standard deviations from the mean. At least 89% of all scores will fall within three standard deviations from the mean.

Standard Error of the Mean: The standard deviation of all possible sample means.

Standard Normal Distribution: A normal distribution with a mean of 0 and a standard deviation equal to one.

Statistic: A measured characteristic of a sample.

Statistics: The collection, organization, analysis, interpretation, and prediction of data.

T Distribution: Theoretical, bell-shaped distribution used to determine significance of experimental results based on small samples. Also called the Student t distribution.

T Test: Significance test that uses the t distribution.

Test Statistic: Used in hypothesis testing, it is the sample statistic based on the sample data.

Two-tailed Test of Significance: Any statistical test in which the critical region is divided into the two tails of the distribution. The null hypothesis usually is that a variable is equal to a certain quantity.

Type I Error: The mistake of rejecting the null hypothesis when it is true.

Type II Error: The mistake of failing to reject the null hypothesis when it is false.

TEST YOUR RESEARCH ACUMEN

1. Descriptive Statistics   A) The consistency in which the same results occur.

2. Ex Post Facto   B) Experimental studies that are not "double-blinded" and might cause bias on the part of the researcher.

3. Inferential Statistics   C) A mode of inquiry in which a theory is proposed and hypotheses are made in advance of gathering data about a specific phenomenon. Hypothetical -deductive theory.

4. Factorial Design   D) A form of descriptive research in which the investigator looks for relationships that may explain phenomena that have already taken place.

5. A Priori   E) A method used to depict systematically the facts and characteristics of a given population or area of interest.

6. Validity   F) Differences in independent variables relevant to a study are controlled.

7. Reliability   G) A method that rigorously explores the efficacy of a program, treatment, or product.

8. Rosenthal Effect   H) A method used to study the effects of more than one independent variable on more than one dependent variable.

9. Hawthorne Effect   I) A set of procedures used to test hypotheses or estimate the parameters in a population.

10. Quasi-Experimental   J) Subjects appear to make progress *just* because they are subjects.

11. Covariant Analysis   K) A method in which a sample of convenience is used and then treated to determine if there is any significant differences pre and post treatment.

12. Evaluative Research   L) The extent to which data measure what they purports to.

Ans.: 1- E, 2-D, 3-I, 4-H, 5-C, 6-L, 7-A, 8-B, 9-J, 10-K, 11-F, 12-G

The 4 P's
Preliminary Preparation: Proposal Planning
(A recipe for the construction of a dissertation research proposal)

Before you actually do your research, most graduate programs require that you first put together a research proposal. When done properly, this can provide you with a plan and most of the ingredients you will need to complete a high quality dissertation. Most universities require that you submit a three-chapter proposal which can later be transformed (with some modification) into the first three chapters of your dissertation.

A dissertation proposal must contain sufficient detail to convince faculty readers that the proposed investigation: 1) has potential to contribute valuable knowledge to the field; 2) is sufficiently planned to assure that the project can be completed (answers research questions) as described in the proposal document; and 3) will possess the level of intellectual rigor commonly expected at the graduate level of study.

In the proposal you will discuss things that you *are going* to do (use the future tense); in the dissertation you write about things you have done (past tense). According to Dr. Robert E. Hoye of Walden University, "the most important aspect of writing a proposal is the need to ensure that all of the parts of the proposal fit together. You cannot change your methodology without adjusting the purpose and the significance. The review of literature has to be related to the problem and the hypothesis."

Warning! Any time you change one thing in your proposal (or dissertation) you must make sure than any other part(s) of your design with which it is associated is (are) appropriately modified.

In Phase 3 we will examine how to "cook up" both a terrific proposal (what you will do) and a "delicious" dissertation (what you did do). Many of the suggestions presented here were first seen in Phase 1.

PHASE 3

```
PHASE 3

THE FEAST
(Your   Dissertation/Research   Paper)

CHAPTER 1
Appetizer
(Introduction)
CHAPTER 2
Soup/Salad
(Research   Review)
CHAPTER 3/CHAPTER 4
Main   Course
(Methodology   and   Presentation)
CHAPTER 5
Dessert
(Conclusions   and   Recommendations)
```

The   Feast

You are now ready to skillfully dish out a fastidiously prepared feast for your distinctive guests to delectably digest.

As you carefully follow the directions in PHASE 3 of your Dissertation Cookbook, and you present the research that you have done you will be describing to your readers: the importance and background of your problem and the way others have examined this problem. You will describe how you examined this problem and why you chose this method of inquiry. Finally, you will explain the fruits of your investigation and the recommendations that you want to make to others who will be contributing to the future solution or understanding of this problem.

Chapter 1

APPETIZER

1/2 c	Introduction	1 c	Hypotheses
1/4 c	Problem Statement	1 t	Irony
2 c	Background	5 t	Creativity
1/2 c	Purpose	1 t	Drama
1 c	Significance	2 t	Definitions
1.5 c	Nature of study		

Combine all ingredients together carefully in a word processor. Simmer over all thoughts until mixture comes to a boil, stirring frequently with inspiration and ingenuity.

1/2 c   Introduction

The purpose of an Introduction Section is to capture the attention of the reader or set the stage for the courses to follow. An Introduction Section will acquaint the reader with the problem you are studying, the approach that you have chosen to study the problem, and your style of writing. It is the place where your begin to "dish" out your ideas and get your reader's "appetite whetted." An introduction gives the reader a **PEAC** (peek) at your study. It usually:

1. **P**uts your study in some perspective.
2. **E**stablishes the need for your study.
3. **A**lerts the reader to what will follow.
4. **C**atches the attention and interest of the reader.

As suggested by the proportion, 1/2 c, the actual introduction to your study is usually brief (one or two pages). Below you will find some attention-getting ways to introduce the reader to your study, and thus, begin your research paper.

___1. A dramatic illustration of the problem. Consider the worst case scenario of the problem you are investigating or the best case scenario if this problem did not exist.

___2. A quote from a passage that capsulizes the problem. Share with the reader a study that calls attention to the problem you have researched or a quotation from a famous person that supports, or contradicts, your point of view.

___3. A narration describing how your interest in the problem was first piqued and how your convictions have changed since you became aware of the problem and have conducted your study.

FOR YOUR INFORMATION AND EDUCATION:

Most research papers and, thus, dissertations are written in the past tense and in the third person. When relating an anecdotal story or a personal observation, it is usually proper etiquette to say: "the researcher found" in lieu of "I find..."

cutting board:

1. Which of the methods (1-3) above would you be most comfortable using in your introduction?_____

2. Put yourself in the position of the reader. What about this study would capture your interest? Why is it important?

_____

_____

3. On a separate piece of paper, do a mind map of your introduction and attach it here:

1/4 c   The Problem Statement

The Problem Statement Section is the heart of the research paper. The mind seems to follow its own equivalent of Newton's law of inertia and becomes aroused to intense analysis only when some dilemma presents itself. Systematic thought, it seems, is driven by failure of established ideas, by a sense that something is wrong, by a belief that something needs closer attention, or by old ideas and methods which are no longer adequate.

The scope of your study, its ability to make a point, and the amount of research you need to do to make that point depend heavily on the initial specification of the problem or problems under investigation. The Problem Statement Section deals with the reality of the problem you are investigating, or the necessity of a program you are analyzing. The objective of a problem statement is:

1. To persuade your reader that the project is feasible, appropriate, and worthwhile, and

2. To capture and maintain your reader's attention.

The research methodology being employed often helps to dictate what the problem statement is. The following are drafts of potential problem statements that can be used in conjunction with the research methodologies specified for investigating the relationship between *socioeconomic class and education*. It is important that references and citations be included in the actual problem statement when appropriate.

Historical Research: Following the Civil War, .

children from the low socioeconomic strata of our society have been perceived as "less intelligent" by their teachers. Such perceptions have had a disastrous effect on children in this group [example and reference to be supplied]. It is imperative that a study be conducted to determine what about the Civil War has caused this problem to arise?

Evaluative Research: The government program, <u>Headstart</u>, seeks to afford children of low socioeconomic classes in our society an opportunity to increase the chances of their success in school by providing an enriched experiential background. It is important to determine if these lofty goals have been met. [Note: the implication is that if Headstart does what it purports to do, it should be continued and even expanded].

Correlational Research: Children from the low socioeconomic strata of society may be denied proper education because teachers perceive them to be "less intelligent." It is imperative that a study be conducted to determine if there is a relationship between a teacher's perception of a students ability and the quality of instruction administered.

Check to see if your Problem Statement, which you developed in Phase 1, seeks an answer to one or more of the questions listed below:

My research determined or examined:

___1. What is wrong with society, or with one of its institutions, that has caused this problem or allowed this problem to exist?

___2. What has failed in society which has caused this problem?

___ 3. What is missing in society that has allowed this problem to develop?

___ 4. What happened that has become interesting and important enough to study?

___5. What historical description of an event has become open to reexamination?

___ 6. A program that was in need of study, evaluation, or analysis.

___7. A need to develop a program which could contribute to society or one of its institutions.

___8. A need to analyze a current theory in light of new events.

___9. A relationship between the problem and a factor or factors that could be contributing to the problem.

Despite this lengthy description of how to develop the Problem Statement here, and in Phase 1, the statement itself, when complete, should be relatively brief (one or two paragraphs). There is much to think about, but not a great deal to write. In fact, as long as it adequately conveys what you intend, the shorter the problem statement the better.

cutting board:

    1. Which of the question(s) above does your study address?
_____

    2. What research methodology best describes your study? (Check back to PHASE 1-*what's cooking* ?)
_____
_____

    3. In PHASE 1 you created a problem statement prior to the formulation of your topic. Re-write that statement in the space below:
_____
_____
_____

4. Make sure that you have stated the problem precisely and concisely. If that is not the case, rewrite the problem statement with your new insight:

_____
_____
_____
_____

2 c   Background

The brevity of the Problem Statement Section is often offset by the Background Section. Here you will elaborate on why the problem you investigated is of pressing societal concern or theoretical interest. This is the place in your paper where you want to make your reader as interested in the problem as you are and to help him/her understand the need for further elucidation of this problem.

Carefully read the statements below. Put a check next to the ones that apply to your research project and could potentially be used in the Background Section of your paper.

____1. There are knowledgeable observers (political figures, theorists, newscasters, professionals in the field, etc.) who have attested to the importance of this problem.

____2. There are statistics that have attested to the depth and spread of this problem.

____3. The failure of certain aspects of society has made this problem compelling and in need of further examination.

____4. There are theoretical issues that are in need of reexamination. This investigation identified these issues and determined the need for their reexamination.

_____5. There is a particular program or event which is in need of development, investigation, or evaluation.

cutting board:

1. Which statement(s) above pertain to your problem?
_____

2. How will (did) you obtain information to support these statements? (books, videos, articles, consult authorities?)
_____

3. Give at least three reasons why the problem you chose is (was) important and valid to you, society, or some institution in society:
_____
_____
_____

4. If applicable, give at least two concrete examples of the problem:
_____

5. If applicable, what programs have addressed similar issues?
_____

6. To what public statistics, political trends, theoretical controversy does your study relate?
_____
_____
_____

7. What people, besides yourself, have been affected by this problem?
_____

8. How was attention first called to the problem? (Name any key figure or figures that assisted in bringing this problem into focus.)
_____
_____

1/2c Purpose

The Purpose Statement Section deals with the study itself. It describes what you were trying to accomplish by doing your study. Stating the purpose of your study early will focus your reader's attention on the essentials of your project and what it intended to accomplish. Thus, the reader will be better able to judge whether your approach was effective. In most proposals and dissertations, this is about 3/4 of a page. Here you will describe specifically what you intend to find out in your study and why this study is being (has been) conducted.

Put a check next to the phrases that could best be used to complete the statement:

The purpose of this research was to:

____1.   advance knowledge by understanding cause and effect;

____2.   provide new answers to old problems;

____3.   elucidate what makes the program under investigation successful or unsuccessful;

____4.   change a real situation and make it better;

____5.   interpret, evaluate, or analyze existing conditions;

____6.   determine to what extent certain factors contributed to the problem;

____7.   determine the need for a particular program or study;

____8.   describe a problem that has been given little attention up until this point, but could have a great impact on society;

___9. understand why a particular condition exists and who is affected by this condition;

___10. elucidate what aspects of a program are successful and what aspects are not successful.

cutting board:

1. Which of the statements above applies to your study? __

2. State briefly and precisely what your study intends/intended to do about the problem you have specified by completing the following sentence: The purpose of this study was to:

_____
_____
_____

1 c   Significance

Just as the Background Section elaborates on the Problem Statement, the Significance Section elaborates on the Purpose Statement. In the Significance Section you will justify why you chose a particular type of research methodology.

Besides your personal desire and motivation to do research, your wish to obtain a degree, your need for a good grade, and your craving to get something published, there needs to be a more global reason for doing a worthwhile study. You should state who, besides yourself, your immediate family, and close friends, cares that this research was done or not done? This should be about 3/4 of a page explaining why this is such a unique approach and who will be thrilled (beside yourself, your family and friends!) that this study is done. Here is where you tell us what type of contribution you will be making to your profession and the society at large.

The statements below are valid reasons for doing research. Put a check next to the one(s) that apply to your research project and can potentially be used in the Significance Section of your paper.

__1. This study was able to reach people that were not reached by other similar studies. (i.e., a different population was studied).

__2. This study gave a different perspective on an established problem.

__3. This was an appropriate approach to this particular research problem although it had not been embraced before.

__4. There was an important benefit to doing the study this way so that there could be a better understanding of the problem.

__5. If this study was not done, some aspect of society would have been in danger.

__6. This was the first time the problem was examined in this vein.

___7. This study has the potential to effect social change.

___8. This program was needed to rectify certain wrongs in society.

___9. This study provided an objective measure of the success of a particular program.

cutting board:

1. Which statement(s) above pertain to your study? ____
2. State in your own words why this study is important.

_____

_____

3. To whom is your study important, other than yourself?

_____

4. How will society, or the understanding of a particular theory or a particular program, benefit from your study?

_____

5. How would you respond (in a nice way) to a person who says, "So what" to your project?

_____

6. How would you provide a persuasive rationale to the person who says, "so what?"

_____

_____

7. Write down several reasons why you chose to study the problem in this way:

_____

_____

1.5 c Nature of the Study

The Nature of the Study Section (about 2-3 pages) can also be called the research design section. This will be the place where the methodology you used is distinguished from other research methodologies which have been done, or could be done, to investigate this problem or program. It is the "blueprint" of your study, and places your study with similar types-- case study, historical, correlational, evaluative, phenomenological, experimental, or quasi-experimental. In this section you will elaborate on the methodology you have chosen, and justify why this is (was) such a great way to investigate this problem. If you use qualitative research methods you will probably need to do a little more explaining than if you choose (chose) a quantitative design. Provide details on your theoretical framework.

In Phase 1 we discussed different types of research methodologies. Refer to this section now and then answer the questions on the cutting board.

cutting board:

1. From what perspective did you view your problem: past, present, or future? _____

2. Which subset(s) of the past, present, or future perspective seemed to apply the most to your study? [e.g., descriptive, correlational, ground theory, action, heuristic, etc.]
_____

3. Within the perspective of 1 and 2 above, which of the following do (did) you do:

a) describe facts b) suggest causes c) analyze changes
d) investigate relationships e) test causal hypotheses
f) evaluate efficiency or effectiveness g) develop a
program h) develop a theory
_____

4. To summarize, complete the statement below: The methodology that I used in my study could best be classified as a (an)
_____ study because I: _____
_____
_____
_____

5. Name another type of methodology that could have been used to study the problem:
_____

6. Why did you reject this methodology?
_____
_____
_____

1 c   Hypotheses/ Research Questions

In the Hypotheses or Research Questions Section of your dissertation you will elaborate on what you thought you would find prior to doing your study. A research hypothesis is a conjectural, declarative statement of the results you expect to find. Research hypotheses are sometimes referred to as working or substantive hypotheses. They are usually directional, that is a researcher might believe something is more or less than a certain accepted notion or condition. Research questions tend to be more open and probative in nature and state the intent of the study.

There is a difference between a **substantive hypothesis** and a **statistical hypothesis**. The former speculates, somewhat informally, on what you assumed your study would reveal. The later is a formal, testable conjecture which can be translated into mathematical symbols.

Example of a substantive hypothesis: Teachers who have integrated calculators into their own personal lives are more likely to use calculators in their classrooms than teachers who rarely use calculators.

Example of statistical hypotheses:

Ho: There is no relationship between teachers using calculators in the classroom and using calculators every day.

$$r = 0$$

and the alternative hypothesis:

H1: There is a relationship between teachers using calculators in the classroom and using calculators every day.

$$r \neq 0$$

Note: Statistical hypotheses [as discussed in Phase 2] usually come in pairs (the null or no change hypothesis, and the alternative or opposite hypothesis), and are expressed symbolically. Statistical tests are designed to accept or reject (fail to accept) the null hypothesis.

In Chapter 1, only the substantive hypotheses or your expectations need to be expressed (statistical hypotheses belong in Chapter 3).

Check the phrase(s) below that best complete(s) the following sentence: I believed that my study would disclose:

___1. The extent to which this problem affects society or one of its institutions.

___2. The true extent and/or nature of the problem.

___3. A new interpretation to an old problem.

___4. That the program (or treatment) evaluated was effective (or ineffective).

___5. A significant relationship between the factors scrutinized and the problem under investigation.

___6. A need to make a change in an attitude/condition.

___7. Conditions that exist which contribute to the problem studied.

___8. Specific conditions that exist as a result of the problem studied.

___9. One program is more effective than another program.

___10. There is a need for a particular study or program.

cutting board: :

State as clearly and succinctly as possible what you expect(ed) the results of your study to show:

_____

_____

1/2 c Scope an Limitations

In the Scope and Limitations Section (about 2-4 paragraphs) you will delineate special characteristics of your sample and the population from which it comes. For example, a study about education in California would not necessarily be applicable to other geographic regions. If the population is a sample by convenience and not randomized then it cannot be generally applied to a larger population -- only suggested. If you are looking at one aspect, say achievement tests, then the information is only as good as the test itself. You can also give a philosophical framework, like constructivism, to limit the study.

Note: When you are elaborating on the nature of your study and/or on the scope and limitations of your study you might wish to discuss your:
> **Ontology** -- How do you, the researcher view reality; objectively? subjectively? a combination of the two?
> **Epistemology** -- What methodology(ies) will (did) you use to derive, elicit, and analyze data?
> **Theory** -- What interrelated constructs, definitions, and propositions will (did) you use to present a systematic view of the phenomena you are studying? You need to specify relations among variables with the purpose of describing, explaining, and predicting the phenomenon you are studying.

2 T. Definitions

If you are using words in an unusual way, or you are employing words that have more than one definition, it is important that you set aside a section of your first chapter to define these terms. You may define a term operatively: that is, how the definition is being used in relation to your research.

By understanding how you are using the term, the reader will be able to understand your research and appraise it objectively. Formal definitions consists of three parts: the term being defined, the general class to which the concept being defined belongs, and the specific characteristics that distinguish the term from other members of the class.

For example, a study on alternative learning might include: for the purpose of this study, "*distance education* refers to imparting knowledge where the learner and the facilitator are at different locations. "

Before you go much further in your writing, it is important to understand the high level of quality that will need to go into your final proposal and dissertation. The issues of quality writing and editing were the focus of ASGS *Thesis News* no. 2 (1997) which contends that: "Writing standards and proper formatting have increased in importance as computers allow both easier editing and even more sophisticated desk-top publishing. Advisors are simply unwilling to accept misspelled or ungrammatical writing when spellchecks and grammar checks are built-in-features of most word programs. (p 2)."

CHAPTER 2
Soup/Salad
[Research Review]

An acronym for what The Research/Literature Review Chapter does is **LEADS**; for it "leads" the reader to the understanding of how your study fits into a larger picture of things, how others have dealt with and been affected by the problem, and why you chose to study the problem the way you did.

LEADS

1 c   **L** ays the foundation for the study.
2 c   **E** lucidates the problem.
1 c   **A** nalyzes why your study is appropriate.
1 c   **D** escribes why your study is capable of solving the problem.
1 c   **S** hows studies similar to yours.

The Literature/Research Review chapter is one of the most important parts of your dissertation. It describes in detail other studies that have been done that have dealt with the same or similar problems. It puts your research into a set with other studies and documents that have dealt with comparable issues. It gives you the knowledge to become an expert in the area that you are investigating. A thorough review of the literature also safeguards against undertaking a study that may have already been conducted, may not be feasible to do, or might not be of much value when set against what needs to be researched in a particular field.

Check back to Phase 1 in your Dissertation Cookbook's *read efficiently section* to make sure that you are effective in your probing for information. Although there is no set rule on "how many" sources you need to consult for your dissertation, most chefs tend to review between 60 and 100 studies and or programs that are related to their topic, and most literature/research review's constitute about 1/4 to 1/2 of the written research paper. These numbers will vary depending on:

1. How unique your study is.

2. How far back in time you choose to go.

3. How you define the "related" topics.

Just as there are restaurants which only serve soup and salad, the research/ literature review itself could be your study. This is often the case if the intent of the research is to present a "meta-analysis" of research that has been conducted on a specific topic such as violence among youth.

In the Research/Literature Review Chapter you will slowly illuminate on how careful you were in preparing your exemplary "meal" and how familiar you are with the previous works that have been done in this area. As your readers "nibble" on the information you adeptly "dish out," you can unveil in this chapter why you chose your main course, why you decided to serve the meal the way you did, and why the utensils you chose were appropriate for this type of feast. Keep in mind that every reference should clearly relate to your study, and that subsections are needed to present similar studies and organize your review.

Note: A research/literature review is not a book report or a string of annotated bibliographies. It is a critical analysis of other peoples research and how their research relates to your study, and it is presented as a cogent whole.

Evaluating a source can begin even before you have the source in hand. You can initially appraise a source by first examining the bibliographic citation-- a written description of a book, journal article, essay, or some other published material. Bibliographic citations characteristically have three main components: author, title, and publication information. These components can help you determine the usefulness of this source for your paper.

• Recipe for Appraising an Author

1. What are the author's credentials--educational background, past writings, or experience--in this area? Is the book or article written on a topic in the author's area of expertise?

2. Have you seen the author's name cited in other sources or bibliographies? Respected authors are cited frequently by other scholars. For this reason, always note those names that appear in many different sources.

3. Is the author associated with an institution or organization? What are the basic values or goals of the organization or institution?

• Check the Date of Publication

1. When was the source published? This date is often located on the face of the title page below the name of the publisher. If it is not there, look for the copyright date on the reverse of the title page. On Web pages, the date of the last revision is usually at the bottom of the home page, sometimes every page.

2. Is the source current or out-of-date for your topic? Topic areas of continuing and rapid development, such as technology, demand more current information. On the other hand, topics in the arts often require material that was written many years ago.

• Check the Edition or Revision

Is this a first edition of this publication or not? Further editions indicate a source has been revised and updated to reflect changes in knowledge, include omissions, and harmonized with its intended reader's needs. Also, many printings or editions may indicate that the work has become a standard source in the area and is reliable.

- Check the Publisher

If the source is published by a university press, it is likely to be scholarly. Although the fact that the publisher is reputable does not necessarily guarantee quality, it does show that the publisher may have high regard for the source being published.

- Check the Title of Journal

Is this a scholarly or a popular journal? This distinction is important because it indicates different levels of complexity in conveying ideas. If you need help in determining the type of journal, you may wish to check your journal title in the latest edition of Katz's Magazines for Libraries (Uris Ref Z 6941.K21 1995) for a brief evaluative description.

Keyword searching is a powerful and flexible way to find books, periodicals, and other materials on-line. A keyword search looks for any word or combination of words in the author, title, and subject fields of data bases. Keyword searches use connectors to search for two or more words in specific ways. The three most useful connectors are AND, OR, and ADJ. AND specifies that both words must appear somewhere in the document, thus NARROWING your search. OR specifies that either word may appear in the record, ADJ specifies that the words must be adjacent and in the same order, thus guaranteeing that the words are searched AS A PHRASE. This can also be accomplished using quotation marks: "child psychology" works the same as child adj psychology.

The questions below can be used to describe and assess the merits of previous studies and could be included when writing the Literature/Research Review in your research paper. It is unlikely that any one study will provide the answers to all these questions, but the questions can serve as a guideline for critical reviews.

1. What was done? Was it effective?

2. When did this take place? What was the accepted belief at this time? Are things different now?

3. Where did this study or event take place?

4. Who was involved?

5. What methodologies were used?

6. What were the limitations? How were these limitations addressed?

7. What type of instruments were used?

8. What was the sample and population studied?

9. What did this add to the knowledge or solution of the problem?

10. What recommendations were made?

11. Who was affected by this study or program?

12. What are the similarities between this study and your study?

13. Was this an appropriate means of dealing with the problem?

14. How is this different from your study?

According to Simpson (1989) A literature review functions as a means of conceptualizing, justifying, implementing, and interpreting a research investigation. Without a literature review it is impossible for others to ascertain the significance of your study and how it will contribute to the knowledge base of a field.

cutting board:

1.   As you examine articles, textbooks, speeches, video presentations, web pages, documentaries, etc., that are related to your topic and the problem you are investigating, determine which of the questions delineated were addressed and which should have been addressed. Elaborate on other issues that the materials dealt with related to your problem or topic.

2.   Take good notes and after a "reasonable" amount of information has been obtained, enter it into your computer, journal, tape deck, or typewriter. If you take notes ON your computer you will save a great deal of time.   These transcribed notes are the ingredients for your Literature/Research Review Chapter, Chapter 2, of your dissertation.

3.   In the space below, write down key words that are closely related to your research.

_____
_____
_____
_____
_____
_____
_____
_____

4.   Remember to write down the following information, if applicable, after you have examined a source:

Author, publisher, city of publisher, copyright date, title, page number, name of periodical, date, volume number, quotes you plan to use, page number of quotes.

CHAPTER 3
1/2 Main course
[Methodology--what did you do?]

Congratulations! Now that you have reached this point in your Dissertation Cookbook, you are ready to put together many of the ingredients that you have carefully amassed in PHASES 1 and 2 and create a splendid main course.

The cutting board activity that follows can be used to prepare a delicious and nutritious Chapter 3 in a jiffy. For your proposal this is usually 4-8 pages; in your dissertation it is usually 10-25 pages. In qualitative studies this is usually 25-50 pages.

cutting board:

From PHASE 2 obtain the following information:

1. What population did you study?
_____

2. How did you choose your sample? (What criteria did you use?) How did you contact your subjects or obtain the documentation you needed?
_____

3. How large was your "n" (How large was your sample?) __

4. Classify your study. (Look at the *What's Cooking Section* and inform the reader about the type of research methodology you used.)

_____

5. Why did you choose this type of methodology?
_____
_____

6. What type of instrument(s) did you use?

_____
_____
_____

7. Why did you choose these types of instruments?

_____
_____
_____

8. Explain any means you had of knowing the instruments were valid and reliable:

_____
_____
_____

9. Describe (in great detail) the procedure you used to administer your instruments and obtain your data.

_____
_____
_____

10. Who else was involved in this aspect of the study?

_____

11. Explain any special things you needed to do to see that the information you sought was obtained and reliable.

_____

12. If you did a pilot study, what information did you obtain from that inquiry? _____

_____
_____
_____

13. What were your statistical hypotheses?

_____
_____
_____
_____

14. Describe how you tested your hypotheses?

_____
_____
_____

15. If you used a statistical package on a computer, what program was it? _____ Why did you choose it? _____

16. Describe any problems or snags that you encountered while obtaining your data.

Each sub-section of Chapter 3 should be highlighted in some way. You want to convince the reader that you have (had) a well thought out plan to *collect, organize, analyze, and interpret data.* You must convince the reader that you can (have) achieve(d) the purpose of your study.

As mentioned earlier, it is usually easier to use an instrument that has an established "cooking" record than to create your own. This means that it has probably already been shown to be both valid and reliable. However, if you have created your own instrument for data collection, then you must describe what you have done to see that it is valid (does what it purports to do) and how you know it is reliable (consistent). Panels of experts, pilot studies, and content analysis can help in this respect. You must explain how you know the data you collected was reliable and valid.

Stir and fry all the ingredients together and arrange them in a pleasing and delectable manner and you will have 1/2 of your main course and Chapter 3 of your dissertation complete! Savor the taste.

CHAPTER 4
other 1/2 of Main Course
[Presentation and Analysis of Data]

Here is where you provide the "punch" line or tell the reader what you discovered from your study. You have already made the preliminary preparation for this Chapter in Phase 2 of your Dissertation Cookbook. You can use that information to guide you through the writing of Chapter 4 of your dissertation.

The Presentation and Analysis Chapter of your dissertation usually contains many of the "garnishings" listed below. Check each "ingredient" that you plan to include. (Once you have successfully incorporated a particular component into the body of your paper, acknowledge that accomplishment by highlighting that task with a colorful pen.)

___1. A detailed description of the data uncovered. (include means, percentages, standard deviations, **t** or **z** values, rho values, chi square values, p values, alpha values, ANOVA, etc.)

___2. Tables and graphs depicting your data.

___3. The results of your hypothesis testing.

___4. The statistical significance of your findings.

___5. A summary of any interviews that you conducted.

___6. Any observations that you or a research assistant made in relationship to the problem.

___7. If you used surveys or tests explain how each item was "weighted" and how it was used to help you arrive at your conclusions.

The more conventional your analysis, the less detail you may need to provide, because the meaning of what you are doing will be more obvious to your reader. You do not, e.g., need to give a lengthy definition of what a delphi study is. Instead, you should explain how you used delphi techniques to evaluate your data. On the other hand, if you are doing something *unusual* you should build the case for its legitimacy here.

cutting board:

Carefully examine the following sample prospectus, and then carefully put together a prospectus for your research proposal. Make sure you share this with the members of your committee and those who will be closely involved with approving your research.

Sample Blue Print(prospectus) for a Proposal

The application of the 12 step programs by alcoholics who have been successful in after care.

Problem Statement: Alcohol abuse is one of the most critical problems facing society today (citation). The 12 step program has been purported to be the primary model for treatment of alcoholism (citation).

Yet, to date, there has been little, if any, formal evaluation of the actual use and application of this program for those who are able to maintain abstinence. In order to provide the most effective and expeditious treatment for alcoholics, it is imperative that a study be done to determine to what extent the 12 step program has been utilized by those who have been successful in aftercare.

Introduction. Quote from Kaminer; I'm Dysfunctional You're Dysfunctional, questioning the efficacy, and discussing the overuse, of the 12 step program.

Purpose: The purpose of this study will be to evaluate a group of successful participants in alcoholics anonymous with respect to their degree of use of the 12 steps of Alcoholics Anonymous. Since the 12 step program is hailed as the paramount means of successfully treating those suffering from chemical dependency, it is imperative that a study be conducted to ascertain the actual use of the program by those who have been successful in care.

Research Question: To what extent is the 12 step program being used by those who have been successful in aftercare?

Significance: This study will be able to reach people who have not been reached before. The researcher will elaborate on his personal qualifications to obtain the desired information. If the study reveals that successful patients practice only part of the program then this information could aid counselors in seeking a more concentrated and abridged treatment regime, thus saving patients, their families, and society, time and money.

Background: 12 step program development; alcoholism as a disease; alcoholism and society; cost of treatment.

Nature of the Study: A combination of ethnographic case study and evaluative study. The researcher believes that in order to elicit accurate information from this population, the

---

investigator must have personal knowledge of this disease. The researcher plans to discover what the subjects believe or perceive they have experienced. The investigator further believes that nothing can be understood apart from the context within which it was experienced.

<u>Literature Review:</u> After-care, alcoholism, (5 yr. max.). 12 step program; alcohol as a disease; other programs for recovery and treatment of substance abuse; evaluation of other recovery programs. [Proposal-- 10-20 pages; Dissertation-- 50-70 pages.]

<u>Scope and Limitation:</u> The subjects in this study are graduates of an alcoholic treatment center in Southern California and all reside in the Southern California area. The social conditions and anti-alcohol campaigns that are prevalent in this geographic region might not exist in other areas of the nation.

<u>Methodology</u>: The researcher is trying to determine how the 12 step program is actually being utilized. The population to be studied is alcoholics who have maintained sobriety for at least one year. The sample will come from graduates of an outpatient alcohol treatment center in Southern California, and will include approximately 25 men and 25 women, ages 20 to 60. Subjects will be selected with the help of personnel from the center based on the willingness of patients to participate in the study. The researcher will use a questionnaire designed by experts in the area, and conduct personal interviews. Questionnaire will make use of visual analog scale with multiple means of assessing the utilization of each step of the 12 step program. The instruments will be validated by a panel of experts in the field. Permission to do study will be obtained. The research will determine which of the 12 steps is most likely to be utilized by all by gender and by age. Using descriptive statistics, the researcher will report on the step(s) that are most utilized by the group as a whole and by other criteria such as age and gender. The researcher will attempt to determine if their is a linear correlation between gender, ethnic group, age, occupation, and other factors and rankings of the 12 steps by the frequency of their use, using non-Parametric statistics and multiple correlational hypothesis testing.

<u>Definition:</u> sobriety, abstinence, 12 step program, aftercare

<u>Social impact of Study</u>- Perhaps crime, caused by alcoholism could be curtailed if there was an effective treatment for alcoholics. In this day of instant everything, there is a constant search to condense and distill effective programs for the most expeditious implementation. If this study shows that certain steps in the 12 step program are not utilized by successful patients, then an investigation of those steps might be studied in greater detail to determine their fruitfulness.

cutting board:

Present your own prospectus on your research proposal to share with the members of your committee and those who will be evaluating your research.

Proposal Outline--Blue Print--Prospectus

Study Title:

Problem Statement: (Write in full)

Introduction: (sketch)

Purpose: (sketch)

Significance: (sketch)

Limitations/Scope: (write in full)

Background: (sketch)

Nature of the Study: (select type(s))

Definitions: (list of words)

Literature Review: (areas to investigate)

Methodology:

    Research questions and/or hypotheses:

    Population/sample:

    Instrument(s) (how to show: validity? reliability?)

    data-- How will you:
          Collect data?
          Organize data?
          Analyze data?
          Interpret data?
          Make predictions?

Social Impact: (give details)

CHAPTER 5
Dessert
[Conclusions, Implications, and Recommendations]

Kudos, cheers, and compliments to the "chef." It is now time to relax and savor the final moments of your eloquent banquet. Here is the time where you can editorialize about your study and advise future cooks on how to cultivate similar feasts.

Put a check next to each item that you plan to serve for dessert:

___1. A summary of what your study found.

___2. An editorial on what your findings mean to the population you studied.

___3. A discourse on how your findings will affect society in general.

___4. Suggestions to others on how to serve a similar feast at a future banquet.

___5. Advice on what can be done to solve the problem in light of your findings.

___6. A list of things that need closer examination in light of your findings.

___7. An opinion on how effective the program, product, or treatment you studied was in meeting its goals and how you would like to see change made in the future.

___8. Suggestions on how the program or treatment that you developed will, or could, be implemented while speculating on the anticipated results.

_____ 9. What you might have done differently with the benefit of hindsight.

_____10. What further study will most likely need to be done now that yours is complete?

_____11. Who needs to pay attention to the results of your study and how will that information be given to them?

_____12. How will the information you obtained effect your sample? population? society?

ABSTRACT
Menu

Most research papers are preceded by an abstract, a brief summary of the research. This serves as a "menu" for your feast. When putting together your abstract make sure you include:

1) a statement of the problem you have investigated.
2) a brief description of the research method and design.
3) major findings and their significance.
4) conclusions and recommendations.

A reader should be able to decide from the abstract whether or not to read the entire dissertation. Since it is not part of the dissertation it should neither be numbered or counted as a page. To fulfill the requirement that the doctoral dissertation be available to other scholars, you or your graduate school generally send(s) a copy of the abstract to University Microfilms, which will print your abstract in Dissertation Abstracts International (DAI). Abstracts published in DAI are limited to a maximum of 350 words.

As for the form and style:

(2.5 cm)

Abstract [or ABSTRACT]

(double space)

Title

(double space)

b y

(double space)

Author

(double space)

Text   (double spaced and about 1.5 pages).

You can now celebrate the birth of an excellent contribution to society and a remarkable repast. You probably want to write "thank you cards" by adding an acknowledgment page after the table of contents to show your appreciation to everyone who helped you create this feast. By writing a well-written, high quality research paper, your scholarly document will most likely be accepted by those who will be assessing it, and your scientific contribution to society will most likely be disseminated.

Thank you for allowing the Dissertation Cookbook to accompany you at this culinary delight. If you know a person who is ABD (All But Dissertation) or someone in need of a guide to successfully complete a research paper, you might want to recommend that they send an e-mail to: **msimon@waldenu.edu**, so that they, too, might have their very own copy of the Dissertation Cookbook.

BON APPETIT!

SUGGESTED READINGS

Fundamentals of Educational Research, Gilbert Sax, New Jersey, Prentice Hall, 1979.

     This work is a practical guide to graduate level research in education. It shows how to select a research project, how to conduct the research, and how to interpret the research. It carries the reader from analysis to presentation of research.

How We Know What Isn't So - The fallibility of human reason in every day life. Thomas Gilovich, New York: Free Press, A division of Macmillan, Inc. 1991

     Gilovich explains in detail the truth to Artemus Ward's famous expression "It ain't so much the things we don't know that get us in trouble. It's the things we know that just ain't so." He examines how questionable and erroneous beliefs are formed, and how they are maintained. Despite popular opinion, people do not hold questionable beliefs simply because they have not been exposed to the relevant evidence, or because they are unintelligent or gullible. Many questionable and erroneous beliefs have purely cognitive origins, and can be traced to imperfections in our capacities to process information and draw conclusions. They are not the products of irrationality, but of flawed rationality.

Research Methods in Education, a practical guide, Robert Slavin, New Jersey, Prentice Hall, 1984.

     This text is primarily designed to serve as a basic resource for a course on research methods of education but it can also be used by anyone who expects to conduct social science research. Its intent was to show how to use research designs and procedures to get the best possible answers to the best possible questions. It discusses research design issues in the light of the limitations and realities of institutional settings.

How to Conduct surveys, a step-by-step Guide, Arlene Fink and Jacqueline Kosekoff, Beverly Hills, Ca, Sage Publications, 1985.

     The purpose of this guide is to help the reader organize a rigorous survey and evaluate the credibility of existing surveys. Its aim is for simplicity rather than embellishment.

Research in Education: an Introduction, Bill Turney & George Robb, Hinsdale, Illinois, The Dryden Press Inc., 1971.

     This book deals with issues such as "What constitutes research? What is the scientific approach to research? How do you select and evaluate a research problem? It offers advice on using the library in educational research and discusses in detail techniques and tools of the educational researcher.

Tests, Measurement and Evaluation, a developmental approach, by Arthur Bertrand and Joseph P. Cebula, Addison Wesley CO, Menlo Park, California, 1980.

     The testing movement in America has come under severe criticism in resent years by those who claim that there is too much emphasis on "standardized" instruments to measure intelligence and achievement. Some have even referred to such tests as "dehumanizing" and do not provide accurate assessment of individual differences.

This book takes the view that tests in and of themselves are not dangerous, but feel that when used properly can provide the classroom teacher with a helpful set of assessment tools. It takes a developmental approach to learning and growth, emphasizing the need to understand each developmental stage of physical, cognitive and personal growth and how each stage dramatically affects the others throughout a child's life.

Survey Research Methods, by Floyd J. Fowler, Jr. Sage Publications, Newbury Park, Ca 1988.

The main purpose of this text is to produce a comprehensive summary of current knowledge about sources of error in surveys, in particular, the emphasis on minimizing non sampling errors through question design. It also includes a chapter coding and filing preparation to reflect the current importance of computer-assisted telephone interviewing (CATI) and the direct data entry systems.

Improving Interview Methods and Questionnaire Design, by Norman Bradburn, Seymour Sudman and Associates, Jossey- Bass, inc, San Francisco, California, 1979.

This book presents the results of a research program on "response affects" in surveys conducted by the National Opinion Research Center (NORC), and concentrates on research areas most in need of empirical work. The three major variables that affect response rate delineated by the authors are: the task itself, the characteristics of the interviewer and the characteristics of the respondents. The text not only attempts to describe and measure the response affects that are occurring but also to suggest the procedures that yield the most accurate reporting.

Applying Educational Research, by Walter R. Borg, New York, Longman, inc., 1987.

The main goal of this book is to make the reader an intelligent consumer of educational research. This involves the ability to locate research relevant to a given problem, evaluate such research reports, and interpret the research findings.

The author feels that the useful information that has emerged from educational research is difficult to locate and even more difficult to interpret and to relate to the practical problems that teachers and school administrators must address. They quote a study by Reys and Yeager (1974) that reports 87.5 per cent of in-service teachers never read research articles. He believes this trend must be reversed if teaching is to become a true profession.

Human Inquiry: A source book of New Paradigm Research by Peter Reason and John Rowan, New York, John Wiley and Sons, 1987.

According to the authors, there has been much criticism of orthodox research but few have suggested alternatives. This book covers the philosophy, methodology, and practice of research which is collaborative and experiential. They believe that social science research should be *with* people instead of *on* people.

Elementary Statistics, 6h edition, by Mario Triola, Menlo Park, Ca, Benjamin Cummings Co., 1996.

A user friendly text that does not require a strong mathematics background to be understood. It is an interesting and readable source to familiarize the reader with statistics and statistical methods, and it is even written with a sense of humor.

Thesis News, no. 2 - 1997, by ASGS, Incline Village, NV.
This 24 page document is designed to show the doctoral student how to change a rough draft of a dissertation thesis into a polished draft through editing. Included are sections on: the type of editing advisors should do, basic writing suggestions, and the results of a study on thesis editing.

FURTHER READINGS AND REFERENCES

Adam, B. (1991). *Analogy in science: from a psychological perspective.* NY: P. Lang.

American Psychological Association (1994). *Publication Manual of the American Psychological Association* (4th ed.). Washington, DC: Author.

Bechtel, W. (1993). *Discovering complexity: decomposition and localization as strategies in scientific research.* Princeton NJ: Princeton University Press.

Bernstein, R. (1983). *Beyond objectivism and relativism: science, hermeneutics, and praxis.* Philadelphia, PA: University of Pennsylvania Press.

Bigelow, J. (1990). *Science and research.* Cambridge; New York: Press Syndicate of the University of Cambridge.

Babbie, Earl (1983). *Practicing social research,* (3rd. ed.). Belmont, CA:Wadsworth, Publishing Company Inc.

Barzun, Jacques and Graff, Henry, F. (1977). *The modern researcher,* (3rd. ed.) New York, Harcourt Brace Jovanovich, Inc.

Bogdan, R. C. and Biklen, S. K. (1992). *Qualitative Research for Education: An Introduction to Theory and Methods.* Boston, MA: Allyn and Bacon.

Bogdan, R. and S. Taylor (1975). *Introduction to qualitative research methods.* New York: John Wiley & Sons.

Bruce, R.(1982). Edit yourself: *A manual for everyone who works with words.* New York: W.W. Norton & Company.

Campbell, D & Stanley, J. (1966). *Experimental and quasi-experimental designs for research on teaching.* Rand McNally and Company.

Cooper, H.M. (1989) . *Integrating research: A guide for literature reviews : Applied social research method series* (2nd ed.). Thousand Oaks, CA: Sage Publications, Inc.

Cunningham, J. B. (1993). *Action research and public policy.* Westport, CT: Praeger.

Glaser, B. & Strauss, A. (1967). *The discovery of grounded theory*. Chicago: Aldine Publishing Co.

Goldstein , Martin, & Goldstein, I. (1985). *How we know*. New York: De Capo Press.

Guba, E. (1990). *The paradigm dialog*. Newberry Park, CA: Sage Publications Inc.

Guba, E. & Lincoln, Y. (1989) *Fourth generation evaluation*. Thousand Oaks, CA: Sage Publications, Inc.

Jason, G. J. (1989). *The logic of scientific discovery*. New York: Peter Lang.

Kuhn, T. (1970). *The structure of scientific revolutions*. (2nd ed.). Chicago: University of Chicago Press, 1970.

Leedy, P. (1994). *Practical research: planning and design*. (5th ed.). New York: MacMillan Publishing Co.

Lester, J. (1993). *Writing research papers: A complete guide*. New York: Harper Collins College Publishers.

Lincoln, Y.S. & Guba , E. (1985). *Naturalistic inquiry*. Thousand Oaks, CA: Sage Publications.

Margolis, H. (1993). *Paradigms and barriers: How habits of mind govern scientific beliefs*. Chicago: University of Chicago Press.

Merriam, S, & Simpson, E.. (1995). *A guide to research for educators and trainers of adults*. Malabar, FL: Krieger Publishing Co.

Melroy, J.M. (1994). *Writing the qualitative dissertation: Understanding by doing*. Hillsdale NJ: Lawrence Earlbaum Associates.

Miles, M. & Huberman, A. (1984). *Qualitative data analysis: A source book of new methods*. Thousand Oaks, CA: Sage Publications,

Mitroff & Kilman,R. (1978). *Methodological approaches to social science*. San Francisco, CA: Jossey-Bass.

Moustakis, C. (1967). *Heuristic research.* In J. Bugental (ed.). Challenges of humanistic psychology. New York: McGraw-Hill.

Nagel, R. (1979). *The structure of science,* (2nd ed.) Indianapolis; Hackett Pub. Co.

Patton, M. (1990). *Qualitative evaluation and research methods*. (2nd. ed.). Newberry Park, CA: Sage Publications.

Popper, K. R. (1968). *Conjecture and refutations: The growth of scientific knowledge*. New York: Harper and Row.

Reason, P. & Rowan, J. (1994). *Human inquiry: A source book of new paradigm research*. New York: John Wily & Sons.

Simpson, Edwin, L. (1994). A *guide to research for educators and trainers of adults*. Malabar, FL: Krieger Publishing Company.

Taylor, S.J. & Bogdan, R. (1984). *Introduction to qualitative research methods: The search for meanings*. (2nd ed.). New York: John Wiley & Sons.

Toulmin, S. (1972). *Human understanding*. Princeton, NJ: Princeton University Press.

Triola, M. (1997). *Elementary statistics* (6th ed.). Menlo Park, CA: Addison-Wesley.

Tuckerman, B. (1994). *Conducting education research*. Orlando, FL: Harcourt Brace & Company.

Weber, R.P. (1990). *Basic content analysis : Quantitative applications in the social sciences* (2nd ed.). Thousand Oaks, CA: Sage Publications.

William S. & White, E. (1972). *The elements of style*. (2nd ed.). New York: Macmillan Publishing Co.

Yin, R. (1997). *Case study research design and methods* (2nd ed.). Thousand Oaks, CA: Sage Publications, Inc.

Chi-Square (χ^2) Distribution

Area to the Right of the Critical Value

Degrees of freedom	0.995	0.99	0.975	0.95	0.90	0.10	0.05	0.025	0.01	0.005
1	--	--	0.001	0.004	0.016	2.706	3.841	5.024	6.635	7.879
2	0.010	0.020	0.051	0.103	0.211	4.605	5.991	7.378	9.210	10.597
3	0.072	0.115	0.216	0.352	0.584	6.251	7.815	9.348	11.345	12.838
4	0.207	0.297	0.484	0.711	1.064	7.779	9.488	11.143	13.277	14.860
5	0.412	0.554	0.831	1.145	1.610	9.236	11.071	12.833	15.086	16.750
6	0.676	0.872	1.237	1.635	2.204	10.645	12.592	14.449	16.812	18.548
7	0.989	1.239	1.690	2.167	2.833	12.017	14.067	16.013	18.475	20.278
8	1.344	1.646	2.180	2.733	3.490	13.362	15.507	17.535	20.090	21.955
9	1.735	2.088	2.700	3.325	4.168	14.684	16.919	19.023	21.666	23.589
10	2.156	2.558	3.247	3.940	4.865	15.987	18.307	20.483	23.209	25.188
11	2.603	3.053	3.816	4.575	5.578	17.275	19.675	21.920	24.725	26.757
12	3.074	3.571	4.404	5.226	6.304	18.549	21.026	23.337	26.217	28.299
13	3.565	4.107	5.009	5.892	7.042	19.812	22.362	24.736	27.688	29.819
14	4.075	4.660	5.629	6.571	7.790	21.064	23.685	26.119	29.141	31.319
15	4.601	5.229	6.262	7.261	8.547	22.307	24.996	27.488	30.578	32.801
16	5.142	5.812	6.908	7.962	9.312	23.542	26.296	28.845	32.000	34.267
17	5.697	6.408	7.564	8.672	10.085	24.769	27.587	30.191	33.409	35.718
18	6.265	7.015	8.231	9.390	10.865	25.989	28.869	31.526	34.805	37.156
19	6.844	7.633	8.907	10.117	11.651	27.204	30.144	32.852	36.191	38.582
20	7.434	8.260	9.591	10.851	12.443	28.412	31.410	34.170	37.566	39.997
21	8.034	8.897	10.283	11.591	13.240	29.615	32.671	35.479	38.932	41.401
22	8.643	9.542	10.982	12.338	14.042	30.813	33.924	36.781	40.289	42.796
23	9.260	10.196	11.689	13.091	14.848	32.007	35.172	38.076	41.638	44.181
24	9.886	10.856	12.401	13.848	15.659	33.196	36.415	39.364	42.980	45.559
25	10.520	11.524	13.120	14.611	16.473	34.382	37.652	40.646	44.314	46.928
26	11.160	12.198	13.844	15.379	17.292	35.563	38.885	41.923	45.642	48.290
27	11.808	12.879	14.573	16.151	18.114	36.741	40.113	43.194	46.963	49.645
28	12.461	13.565	15.308	16.928	18.939	37.916	41.337	44.461	48.278	50.993
29	13.121	14.257	16.047	17.708	19.768	39.087	42.557	45.722	49.588	52.336
30	13.787	14.954	16.791	18.493	20.599	40.256	43.773	46.979	50.892	53.672
40	20.707	22.164	24.433	26.509	29.051	51.805	55.758	59.342	63.691	66.766
50	27.991	29.707	32.357	34.764	37.689	63.167	67.505	71.420	76.154	79.490
60	35.534	37.485	40.482	43.188	46.459	74.397	79.082	83.298	88.379	91.952
70	43.275	45.442	48.758	51.739	55.329	85.527	90.531	95.023	100.425	104.215
80	51.172	53.540	57.153	60.391	64.278	96.578	101.879	106.629	112.329	116.321
90	59.196	61.754	65.647	69.126	73.291	107.565	113.145	118.136	124.116	128.299
100	67.328	70.065	74.222	77.929	82.358	118.498	124.342	129.561	135.807	140.169

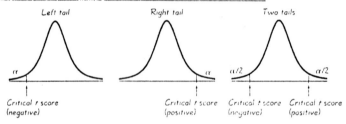

Left tail | Right tail | Two tails

Critical t score (negative) | Critical t score (positive) | Critical t score (negative) Critical t score (positive)

Values of the Pearson Correlation Coefficient

α = .05	α = .01
.950	.999
.878	.959
.811	.917
.754	.875
.707	.834
.666	.798
.632	.765
.602	.735
.576	.708
.553	.684
.532	.661
.514	.641
.497	.623
.482	.606
.468	.590
.456	.575
.444	.561
.396	.505
.361	.463
.335	.430
.312	.402
.294	.378
.279	.361
.254	.330
.236	.305
.220	.286
.207	.269
.196	.256

t Distribution

Degrees of freedom	.005 (one tail) .01 (two tails)	.01 (one tail) .02 (two tails)	.025 (one tail) .05 (two tails)	.05 (one tail) .10 (two tails)	.10 (one tail) .20 (two tails)	.25 (one tail) .50 (two tails)
1	63.657	31.821	12.706	6.314	3.078	1.000
2	9.925	6.965	4.303	2.920	1.886	.816
3	5.841	4.541	3.182	2.353	1.638	.765
4	4.604	3.747	2.776	2.132	1.533	.741
5	4.032	3.365	2.571	2.015	1.476	.727
6	3.707	3.143	2.447	1.943	1.440	.718
7	3.500	2.998	2.365	1.895	1.415	.711
8	3.355	2.896	2.306	1.860	1.397	.706
9	3.250	2.821	2.262	1.833	1.383	.703
10	3.169	2.764	2.228	1.812	1.372	.700
11	3.106	2.718	2.201	1.796	1.363	.697
12	3.054	2.681	2.179	1.782	1.356	.696
13	3.012	2.650	2.160	1.771	1.350	.694
14	2.977	2.625	2.145	1.761	1.345	.692
15	2.947	2.602	2.132	1.753	1.341	.691
16	2.921	2.584	2.120	1.746	1.337	.690
17	2.898	2.567	2.110	1.740	1.333	.689
18	2.878	2.552	2.101	1.734	1.330	.688
19	2.861	2.540	2.093	1.729	1.328	.688
20	2.845	2.528	2.086	1.725	1.325	.687
21	2.831	2.518	2.080	1.721	1.323	.686
22	2.819	2.508	2.074	1.717	1.321	.686
23	2.807	2.500	2.069	1.714	1.320	.685
24	2.797	2.492	2.064	1.711	1.318	.685
25	2.787	2.485	2.060	1.708	1.316	.684
26	2.779	2.479	2.056	1.706	1.315	.684
27	2.771	2.473	2.052	1.703	1.314	.684
28	2.763	2.467	2.048	1.701	1.313	.683
29	2.756	2.462	2.045	1.699	1.311	.683
Large (z)	2.575	2.327	1.960	1.645	1.282	.675

INDEX

alpha values 99
abstract 171
accommodating averages 51
achievement tests, 60
action research 40
ad hoc definitions 52
alternative hypotheses 99
analytic induction 43
analytical scientist 23
ANCOVA 130
ANOVA 107, 110
applied or evaluative research 39
aptitude tests, 60
background 146
bar graph 87
biases 49
bivariate correlation 126
bivariate data 119
candoall model 111
case study 91
causal-comparative research 34
central limit theorem 100
chi-square 117, 132
choline 5
cluster sampling 89
competence 53
conceptual humanist 23
conceptual theorist 22
confidence Levels 92
convenience sampling 90
cause and effect 52
confidence level 102
contingency table 131
contributory 28
correlation 19, 36
correlational Research 144
covariate 130
cover letter 71, 72
critical region 101
critical value 101
cross-sectional 66
deconstruction 47
degrees of freedom 114, 118
Deming 117
delphi 45, 47
demographic 86
dependent variable 108
descriptive research 36
descriptive statistic 88, 94
developmental research 35
distribution-free tests 105

editing 156
equivalence 70
ethics. 48
evaluative research 144
F test 110
faulty comparisons 50
form and style 56
frequency distribution 101
frequency table 85
Gaussian curve 100
geometric mean 51
Gilovitch 32
graphs 52
groundedtheory 43
harmonic mean 51
healthy brain 5
hermeneutics 47
heuristic research 41
histograms 87
historical research 33, 143
holistic research 42
hypotheses 94, 153
I.Q. test 92
independent variables 108, 109, 120
internal consistency 70
interval data 63, 65, 83
interview 75
Introduction 141
keyword searching 160
Kruskal-Wallis (H) 107, 115
kurtosis 85
Likert-type scale 68
longitudinal 66
mean 51, 95
median 51
mind map 13
mode 51
moral and legal issues 53
nature of study 151
nominal data 63, 65, 83
non-parametric 63
non-probability sampling 90
non-response rate 91
null hypotheses 98
objectivity 49
observation 77
ogives 87
one-tailed (right tailed) test 103
ordinal 63, 65, 83
originality 27
p values 99
paired z-tests 109
paired t-test 109
parametric 63, 104

Spearman's rank correlation 122
particular humanist 23
Pearson r 107
personal nterview 75
personality tests or inventories 61
phenomenology 47
pie charts 87
pilot study 71
population, 88
post-hoc comparisons 131
postmodern 47
presentation and analysis of data 165
problem statement 28, 143
psychological tests and inventories 61
pure/basic/experimental research 37
purpose statement 148
qualitative data 116
quality dissertation 156
quality control 117
questionnaires 62
r-squared 122
ratio 63, 64, 66
rational 83
raw" data. 85
regression analysis 120
regression and correlation analysis 119
reliability 69
research methodology 33
research/literature review chapter 157
researchable 26
responsibility 49
runs test. 131
sample 89
sample size 92
sampling error 92
scatter diagram 119
scope an limitations 155
sign test 108
significance section 149
simple random sampling 89
skewness 84
sleep 5
spurious accuracy 50
stability 70
standard deviation 51, 86, 102, 117
standard error of measurement 92
standard error of the mean 102
standard normal distribution 100
statistical hypothesis 82, 153
statistical terms 133
statistics 79
stem and leaf plots 87
substantive hypothesis 96, 153
systematic stratified sampling 89

testing claims 94
tests and inventories 59
Thesis News 156
two-tailed test 103
typology 20
universe 88
validity 70
variable 61, 62
variance 51,86, 117
visualization 3
Wilcoxon rank-sum test 110
Z test 116
z value 100